Jackson COUNTY GEORGIA

Inferior Court Minutes

- 1796-1802 -

(Volume #1)

Compiled by:
Michael A. Ports

Southern Historical Press, Inc.
Greenville, South Carolina

Copyright 2019
By: Michael A. Ports

All rights reserved. No part of this publication may be reproduced, stored in a retrieval system, transmitted in any form, posted On to the web in any form or by any means without the Prior written permission of the publisher.

Please direct all correspondence and orders to:

www.southernhistoricalpress.com
or
SOUTHERN HISTORICAL PRESS, Inc.
PO BOX 1267
375 West Broad Street
Greenville, SC   29601
southernhistoricalpress@gmail.com

ISBN #0-89308-088-8

Printed in the United States of America

Introduction

On February 11, 1796, the Georgia General Assembly created Jackson County from a portion of Franklin County and designated Clarksboro as its first seat of government. In 1801, 40,000 acres of land was set aside for a new state College. Franklin College, now the University of Georgia, began classes the same year, the city of Athens grew up around the school, and the new County of Clarke was formed around it. As a result, the Jackson County seat moved to an old Indian village called Thomocoggan. In 1804, the village was renamed Jefferson, in honor of Thomas Jefferson. In 1811 Jackson County lost more territory to the new Madison County, in 1818 to the new Gwinnett, Hall, and Walton counties, in 1858 to the new Banks County, and in 1914 to the new Bartow County.

The Inferior Court, made up of five elected justices of the peace for the county, tried any civil case, except those involving title to land. The Inferior Court had jurisdiction over all county business matters, such as care for the poor, building and maintaining the courthouse and jail, building and maintaining public roads, bridges, and ferries, issuing licenses to sell liquor, appointing constables and other local officials, nominating justices of the peace, performing naturalizations, appointing guardians, authorizing apprenticeships and indentures, and administering county funds.

The following transcription is taken from the microfilm made at the courthouse in Jefferson on April 16, 1963 by the Genealogical Society of Salt Lake City, Utah and is available at the Georgia Archives in Morrow, Georgia and the Family History Library. The heading on the microfilm roll reads

Inferior Court
Minutes

Sitting for County Purposes
Sitting for Ordinary Purposes

No Index

1796-1802

On the spine of the original volume are the words

Jackson County Inferior Court Minutes 1796-1802

The minutes commence on August 1, 1796 and continue through September 28, 1801. The first volume of original court minutes is not indexed; however, a complete full-name index follows the transcription. The reader should know that a lone surname in the index indicates that no first name appears in the minutes, for example Mr. Smith, Smith & Company, or said Smith. An index entry such as Smith, ___, Sm___, William, or ___, William indicates that an entire name was entered into the minutes, but at least part of it has been obscured by an ink blot, smear, tear, or other imperfection. The pages of the volume are not numbered. To assist the researcher in locating the original pages, the symbol ___ is placed at the bottom left-hand corner of each original unnumbered page. By noting the date, or at least the court term, of an individual entry in the minutes, the researcher should not have too much difficulty in locating that entry in the original record or on the microfilm copy.

Benjamin Easley, Daniel W. Easley, W. Pentecost, and G. Taylor served as clerk during the period covered by the minutes. The clerk frequently signed the minutes at the close of each day's session to certify the accuracy of the minutes as well as attesting to numerous other entries. Based solely upon the different handwriting, at least three or four other persons entered some of the daily proceedings, but their names were not recorded. For the most part, their handwriting is legible, making the transcription straightforward and not too difficult. The occasional ink smear or other imperfection is noted within brackets, for example [smear], [torn], or [illegible]. The transcription follows Sperry's recommended guidelines for reading early American script.[1]

Sometimes the clerks formed the letters "a" and "o" in a very similar manner, making abbreviations such as Jas. and Jos. and surnames Harman and Harmon or Low and Law impossible to distinguish. At other times, the letters "a" and "u" are too similar to differentiate between such names as Burnett and Barnett. The formation of the letters "i" and "e" sometimes makes it difficult to distinguish between such names as Melton and Milton, for example. Also, the clerk formed the capital letters "I" and "J" identically. Determining which letter usually is not a problem when the first letter of a surname, but entirely a guess when a middle initial. Sometimes the clerk crossed the letter "t" by extending the horizontal line across the entire word, making it difficult to distinguish between such surnames as Cutter, Cutler, and Culter or Cotton and Colton. Occasionally, the clerk failed

---

[1] Sperry, Kip. *Reading Early American Handwriting.* Genealogical Publishing Company, Inc., Baltimore, Maryland, Sixth Printing, 2008.

to cross the letter "t" at all, leaving the reader wondering if the name was Jewett or Jewell, for example.

The transcription does not correct any grammar or spelling, no matter how obvious the errors, but does add a few commas, semicolons, apostrophes, and periods for clarity. Finally, the clerk entered a vertical squiggly line to delineate case citations and other headings, duplicated by the symbol } in the transcription. Careful researchers will consult either the original record or the microfilm copy either to confirm the transcription or formulate alternative interpretations of the clerks' handwriting.

Generally, the transcription maintains the overall format of the minutes, but presents the case citations, jury panels, lists of witnesses, and other court proceedings in a standard and consistent format. The minutes contain numerous original signatures, beyond merely those of the judge and the clerk, including those of many attorneys, individuals filing bonds for appeals and stays of execution, and their securities, as well as those subscribing to various oaths.

To the right of many of the original signatures, the clerk entered the capital letters S S enclosed by a squiggly line in the form of a circle or oval as follows

That symbol is not included in the transcription.

In the lefthand margin adjacent to numerous entries, the clerk entered the following symbol whose meaning is not understood.

That symbol also is not included in the transcription.

The book is dedicated to the memory of the author's numerous Georgia ancestors, although none ever were residents of Hancock County during the period covered by the transcription. Many thanks are offered to the kind, patient, and generous staff of the Georgia Archives, for their assistance and suggestions, not only in locating the original records, but in understanding their historical context. Thanks also are offered LaBruce Lucas of the Southern Historical Press for his sage professional advice and counsel. Special thanks are offered to my mother, Ouida J. Ports, who helped instill in me a deep appreciation of American history and genealogy.

Inferior Court Minutes

State of Georgia }
Jackson County }

At a Court began and held in and for the County aforesaid the first day of August 1796.

Present   Joseph Humphries }
                                Absalom Ramey   } Esquires
                                Rod^k Easley   } Judges
                                Montfort Stokes }
                                James Pitman.   }

On Motion of Thos P. Carnes, Att^y for Wm Brown, stating that an Action was depending in the Inferior Court of Franklin County, Wm Brown vs John Barnett, which cause was ordered by said Court to be removed to this, as the defendant resided in this County.

Ordered, that the Clerk enter the same on the docquet and stand for trial next term.

August Term 1796

Then proceded to nominate Constables when David Shay, Samuel Bridgewater, and Johnson Clark was appointed and qualified also John Kennerley, who is to be qualified hereafter.

Ordered, that a road be cut from this place, the nearest & best way, to the Cherokee Corner, and that Samuel Knox, John Heart, & Danl W. Easley be commissioners of the same.

And, that a Road be cut from this place, Meeting a road from Franklin Court House, Ja^s East, Wm Carter, & Obriant Mooney, Commissioners of the same.

Signed   J. L. Humphries
                                Rod^k Easley
                                Ab^s Ramey
                                Ja^s Pitman
                                Wm M. Stokes

The Court adjourned until court in course.

D. W. Easley, Clk

At a Court began & held in and for the County of Jackson 2 Jany 1797.

Present   Joseph Humphries }
                               Absalom Ramey } Esq^{rs}
                               Wm M. Stokes } Judges

The Sheriff returned his Writ of Venire facias and it appeared thereby that the following persons were returned to serve as Jurors the Present Term, to wit.

1. Jno Bradshaw
2. Jno Parks
3. Chesley Morris
4. Ja^s Scott
5. Jno Cuningham
6. Isaac Hill
7. Wm Gentry
8. Ben Vermillion
9. Jordon Anderson
10. Saml Kilough
11. Jno Miller
12. Walter Bell
13. Nathl Medlock
14. Ja^s Harper
15. Wm Duke
16. Ja^s Armstrong
17. Jno Party
18. Jno Reynolds
19. Asa Hamilton
20. Henry Ledbetter
21. Wm Sparks
22. Mathew Moore
23. George Kennerly
24. Randolph Traylor
25. Jessee Sparks
26. Jno Nelson
27. Mathew Waters
28. Mial Barnett
29. David Luckie
30. Jacob Housler
31. Ge^o McFalls
32. Isaac Midlebrook
33. Danl Mathews
34. Wm Cawthorn
35. Henry Trent
36. Miles Gathright
37. Saml Knox
38. Cain Gentry
39. Absalom Halcoor
40. David Kilough
41. Jno Shields
42. Saml Best
43. Thos Kenerly
44. Thos Nelson
45. Danl Williams
46. Wm Ramey

Jany Term 1797

William Brown }
    vs   } Case
John Barnett }

The following Jury Sworn

1. Jn° Bradshaw
2. Jn° Parks
3. Chesley Morris
4. Jn° Cuningham
5. Isaac Hill
6. Ben Vermillion
7. Saml Kilough
8. Jn° Miller
9. Walter Bell
10. James Harper
[blank]
12. Wm Duke

Who returned the following Verdict. We the Jurors find for the defendant a non suit, with Costs of suit.

Ja^s Harper, foreman

Pltf appealed.

Andrew McNabb }
    vs   } Attachm^t
John Kenerly   }

This day appeared in open court John Reynolds & Robert McGowin and acknowledged themselves Special Bail for the defendant in this Case, that is, that the party defendant shall pay the money awarded, that they will do it for him, or surrender up the defendant, in discharge of themselves when he shall be charged

---

in Execution.

Signed   Jn° Reynolds
                                    Robt McGowin

Taken in open Court }
D. W. Easley, Clk   }

John Grisham & }
Elizabeth Scott }
    vs   } Case
Thos & Joshua }
Hightower }

This day appeared in open court Johnson Strong & William Ramey Acknowledged themselves Special Bail for the defendant in this Case, that is that the party defendant shall pay the money awarded, that they will do it for him, or surrender up the defendants, in discharge of themselves when he shall be charged in execution.

Signed   Johnson Strong
                                       Wm Ramey

D. W. Easley, Clk

John Moss }
    vs   } Attachm^t
Laurence Briars }

This day appeared in Court William Strong & acknowledged himself Special

———

Bail for the defendant in this case, that is that the party defendant shall pay the money Awarded, or that he will do it for him, or surrender up the defendant, in discharge of himself when he shall be charged in execution.

Signed   Wm Strong

D. W. Easley, Clk

William Strong, Junr }
    vs   } Case
Samuel Knox }

This day appeared in Court John Barnett & John Cuningham & Acknowledged themselves Special Bail for the defendant in this case, that is that the party defendant will pay the money awarded, or that they will do it for him, or surrender up the defendants, in discharge of themselves when he shall be charged in execution.

      Signed   Jn° Barnett
            Jn° Cuningham

D. W. Easley, Clk

Edmund Alexander }
   vs   } Attachment
Edmund Taylor }

This day appeared in

———

[blank page]

———

Court William Strong & William Ramey and acknowledged themselves Special Bail in this case, that is that the party defendant will pay the money awarded, or that they will do it for him, or Surrender up the defendant, in discharge of themselves when he shall be charged in execution.

Signed   Wm Strong
             Wm Ramey

D. W. Easley, Clk

———

      March 16, 1797

The Court met agreeable to adjournment.

Present   Joseph Humphries }
            James Pitman } Judges
            Absalom Ramey }

Ordered, that Writs of Elections for Justices of the peace be Granted to the following Company districts, to wit, N° 1, 3, 5, 7, & 8.

And that William Hutchinson receive the list of Taxable return for the present year.

Ordered, that Benjamin Reynolds be collector of Taxes for the present year.

Court adjourned.

Jo^s Humphries
Ja^s Pittman
Ab^s Ramey

G. Taylor, pro }
D. W. Easley, Clk }

At a Court began & held in and for the County of Jackson the first day of August 1797.

Present   Joseph Humphries }
,   Absalom Ramey   } Judges
,   James Pittman   }

The Sheriff returned his Writ of Venire facias, and it appeared thereby that the following persons mentioned below were returned to serve as Jurors the present term, to wit.

William Strong, Junr }
    vs   } Case
Saml Knox   }

Jury Sworn.

1. Jonathan Lane
2. David Kilough
3. Wm Nichols
4. John Hopkins
5. Arthur Pattern
6. Jno Dukes
7. Joseph East
8. Henry Williams
9. Ge^o Cuningham
10. Wm Hutchinson
11. Th^o Kilpatrick
12. Wm Streetman

We, the Jurors, find five hundred & seven dollars, with Interest, for Plaintiff.

Wm Hutchinson, F. M.

Jn° Michael, surviving }
partner of Michael & Jones }
     vs } Case
Edmund Taylor }

cont^d by consent.

Basil Jones }
     vs } Case
Augustine Blackburne }

cont^d on Affidavit of def^t Att^y.

Jn° Grisham }
& Eliza Scott }
     vs } Case
Thos & Joshua Hightower }

Cont^d by consent.

~~William Strong, Junr~~ }
     vs } ~~Case~~
~~Samuel Knox~~ }

W. William Strong Senr, et al }
     vs } Slander
Saml Knox }

Cont^d by Affd^t of Def^t.

Mathew Finley }
     vs } Case
Henry Trent }

Cont^d by Affd^t of def^t.

David Kilough }
  vs } Case
Isham Williams }

In this case, the defendant came into Court & confessed Judgment for $101.36, with costs of Suit.

Signed   Isham Williams

[blot] Easley pro D. W. Easley, Clk

———

Andrew McNabb }
  vs } Attach^t
Jno Kenerly }

The death of Plant^f Sugested.

Edmund Alexander }
  vs } Attach^t
Edmund Taylor }

This case stands for trial tomorrow.

Francis Gorden & Co }
  vs } Case
George Mcfalls }

In this case, John Nalls came into Court and Acknowledged himself indebted to the Plaintiff in the Sum mentioned in the Bail Bond, on the Condition that Defendant will pay the Condemnation Money, if any, or render his Body to the Common Jail of this County, or he, John Nalls, will do it for him.

Acknowledged in open Court.   John Nall

D. W. Easley, Clk

———

Francis Gorden & Cº }
     vs   } case
Jnº Miller   }

James Miller came into Court and acknowledged himself indebted to the plaintiff in the Sum mentioned in the Bail Bond, on this Condition that, if the defendant be cast he will pay the condemnation Money, if any, or surrender his body to the common Jail of this County, or he, James Miller, will do it for him.

Acknowledged   }
in open Court.   }   James Miller
B. Easley, pro   }
D. W. Easley, Clk }

David Thurmond }
     vs   } Attachm^ت
Benjamin Knox }

In this case, Saml Knox came into Court and acknowledged himself indebted to the plaintiff in the Sum mentioned in the bail bond,

——

on this condition that, if the Def^t be cast, he will pay the condemnation money, if any, or render his body to the common Jail of this County, or he, Saml Knox, will do it for him.

Acknowledged   }
in open Court.   }   Samuel Knox
B. Easley, pro   }
D. W. Easley, Clk }

Edmund Phillips }
     vs   } Attach^t
Saml Pattern   }

In this case, Arthur Pattern came into Court and Acknowledged himself indebted to the Plaintiff in double the Sum Sued for, on this condition that, if the defendant be cast, he will pay the condemnation money, if any, or Surrender his Body to the common Jail of this County, or he, Arthur Pattern, will do it for him.

Acknowledged in open Court.   Arthur Pattern
D. W. Easley, Clk

W^m McKee, to the use }
of Solomon Pattern   }
    vs   } Case
Thos Kennerly   }

In this case, the defendant confessed Judgment, which is entered on back of process.

The Court adjourned till tomorrow ten O'clock.

B. Easley, pro
D. W. Easley, Clk

The Court met agreeable to adjournment.

Present	Joseph Humphries }
,	James Pittman } Judges
,	Absalom Ramey }
,	Rod^k Easley }

Jno Moss   }
   vs   } Attach^t
Laurence Briars }

In this case, the following award was returned by the Arbitrators, to wit. We, Absalom Ramey, William Duke, & Mathew Stone, Arbitrators, find Laurence Briars due Jno Moss Sixty four dollars &

---

twenty eight cents, with Interest from the 7 Jany 1796, With Costs.

      Signed   Absalom Ramey
            Wm Duke
            Mathew Stone

Whereupon, Ordered, that the award be the Judgment of this Court.

Edmund Alexander }
  vs   } Attach^t
Edmund Taylor }

    In this case, the following Jury was Sworn

  1. Jonathan Lane   7. Joseph East
  2. David Kilough   8. Henry Williams
  3. Wm Nichols   9. Ge^o Cuningham
  4. Jno Hopkins   10. Wm Hutchinson
  5. Arthur Pattern   11. Thos Kirkpatrick
  6. Jno Dukes   12. Wm Streatman

We, the Jury, find for the Plaintiff Eight hundred and fifty seven dollars, without any Interest on the same to this day.

Signed.   Wm Hutchinson, F. Man

David Thurmond }
  vs   } Attachment
Benj^a Knox }

In this case, the suit was dismissed at plaintif cost.

paid.

A Petition from Sundry Inhabitants of this County praying that a road leading from Oglethorpe Court house a direct Cours ~~by~~ by Elijah Hendon, thence along the dividing ridge between the North & middle Oconee into the Cedar Shoal road about or below the wolf pen, Crossing the North Oconee at William Head's, Junr.

Ordered, the Same be cut & Jn° Cuningham, Wm Ramey, & Elijah Hendon be Commissioners of the same.

A Petition of Sundry Inhabitants of this County praying a road be laid out from the County line to Fort Washington, Begining on the County line, where the new road strikes the line that leads from Joshua Browning Ferry.

Ordered, that the said road be laid out, and John Fielder, William Hopkins, & ~~Richard Hopkins be Commrs~~ Michael Cup be Commissioners of the same.

The following persons were appointed & Qualified as Constables, gave their Bonds is filed, to wit.

Elijah Gentry, in Capt Jn° Strong's district
Ben Parr Capt Jesse Sparks "
James Henderson Capt Kirkpatrick "
Ben Rodgers Capt Morrisson "

John Hart rendered an Account for Services done as High Sheriff amounting to forty one dollars. We acknowledge the Same to be Just & shall be paid when appropriations are made. (is paid.)

Ordered, that Writts of Elections for Justices of the peace in Capt Tuttle's district be on the 13th Ins^t. Ge° Haney, Thos Burks, & Nicholas Tuttle Superintend the same at the muster ground of said district.

Wm Strong, Junr }
    vs }
Saml Knox }

In this case, Saml Knox came & prayed an appeal, which was granted on his paying up the cost that had arisen, & John Barnett Acknowledged himself Security, agreeable to the Act in such cases mad & provided.

Acknowledged in open Court.   Jn° Barnett
Ben Easley pro
D. W. Easley, Clk

Ordered, that Tavern License be granted to Rod^k Easley, Esquire for retailing Spiritous Liqours &c.

was done.

The Court Adjourned till tomorrow 10 O'clock.

B. Easley, pro   }
D. W. Easley, Clk }

~~Wednesday~~ Thursday, 3 August

The Court met according to adjournment.

Present   Joseph Humphries }
                                James Pittman   } Judges
                                Absalom Ramey   }
                                Rod^k Easley   }

Ordered, That Tavern licence & Licence for to keep a Ferry across the Oconee river at Fort Mathews be granted to Mathew Stone.

Ordered, That Tavern Licence ~~be granted~~ be Granted to Cain Jentry.

Absalom Ramey came into court and pray^d an order be granted for the binding the Orphan Children of Presley Ramey, to wit, Daniel & Edmund, untill they come to the age of twenty one years. Also Nancy, Sarah, & Fanny untill they arrive at the age of Sixteen, the two Boys to be learnt the art or trade of a House Joiner and all necessary Education that Mechanics require, the Girls to have such education as the Sex require or is usual to give Girls.

Miles Gathright came into court and made it Known that he had an Orphan Child at his house since the twenty seventh of May last, by the name of Elizabeth Hickey, and prays payment for Keeping her. Ordered, that he be paid two dollars & twenty-five cents p^r Month for her Support, from that time untill next Court, which he has promised that he will keep her untill that time for which shall be paid as soon as appropriations are Made.

Ordered, that one sixth ~~of each~~ of the ~~general~~ Tax of each individual be added to the General tax for County uses & the Collector be Served with a copy of this order.

———

Ordered, that the following Rates be Lawful for any Tavern Keeper, retailers of Spirituous Liquors to sell by, and not start a larger sum for any single article than what is here allowed.

			Cents
	for Breakfast of good holesome diet		$ 25
first Table	" Dinner of	d° Warm	37½
Second D°	" Dinner of	d° Cold	25
	" Supper of	d°	25
	" Lodging		10
	" half pint of Jamaica or Westindia Rum		25
	" half pint of North East Rum		18¾
	" half pint of Brandy		18¾
	" half pint of Whiskey		12½
	" horse feed 4 cents for each quart } of Corn or bundle of fother }		
	" feeding & Stabling a horse twenty four } hours with a plenty of Corn & fother }		37½

B. Easley P
Joseph Humphreys
Absalom Ramey
James Pittman

The Court adjourn till Court in Course.

B. Easley, pro
D. W. Easley, Clk

———

The following persons were qualified as Justices of the Peace in their respective districts, to wit.

Joseph East   }   Capt Morison's District
Alex^r Morrison }

John Espy   Capt Kilough's d^o

Joseph McCutchin }   Capt Kirkpatrick's d^o
Thos Kirkpatrick }

Micajah Benge   Capt Strong's d^o

Done in open Court }
Test. D. W. Easley, Clk }

October 5th 1797

The following persons were Qualified as Justices of the Peace, on their producing their Commissions from the Governor, before Jo^s Humphries & James Pittman, Esquires, to wit. Paul Patrick & Randolph Traylor for Capt Sparks' District, also Martin Nall & Jno Mcfalls for Capt Bell's District. William Nall was appointed Constable in Capt Bell's district, he came forward, gave his Bond, and was qualified as Such before Joseph East, Esquire.

Testes. B. Easley, pro
D. W. Easley, Clk

At an Inf^r Court began & held in and for the County of Jackson on the Second day of January 1798.

Present   Rod^k Easley }
                                Ja^s Pittman } Judges
                                Abs^m Ramey }

Francis Gordon & Co }
        vs   } Case
Jno Miller   }

Cost paid.

In this suit, the def⁺ came into Court & confessed Judgm⁺ for the sum of eighty five dolls & seventy one cents, with Interest from the first day of Jany 1794 & cost of suit, with stay of execution (cost excp^t), for twelve Months.

Signed.   Jn° Miller

Test. Thos P. Carnes

On motion of M. Williamson, Att^y for Elizabeth Thomas, minor, it is Ordered, that Richd Sapington be appointed guardian, upon his giving bond, with Security, to the Clerk in the Sum of one thousand doll^s.

Letters of Guardianship Issued the third day of January 1798.

B. Easley, Clk

Bazil Jones   }
  vs   }
Augustine Blackburne }

In this case, the death of the def⁺ having been suggested last Court.

Joseph Humphries, administrator, came into Court & acknowledged himself the rightful administrator, whereupon ordered, that the said Joseph Humphries be made party to the above suit & the Suit be continued as the law directs.

Ja^s Grisham &   }
Eliza Scott   }
  vs   } Case
Thos & Joshua Hightower }

In this case, the following Jury N° 1 were sworn, to wit.

    1. Jacob Houver   7. Wm Jones
    2. Jacob Carter   8. Miles Gathright
    3. Johnson Clark   9. Abner James
    4. Gall^t Runnels   10. Danl Young

5. Martin Gardner   11. Thos Carter
6. Jonathan Lane   12. Jno McCartney

We, the Jury, find for the plaintiff the sum of eighty five dollars, with costs.

Signed   M. Gathright, F. M.

James B. Oliver }
     vs   } Case
Edmund Taylor   }

Nonsuit.

Andrew Jether } $1 p^d to def^t
     vs   } Case
Wm Hopkins }

In this Case, the Def^t came into Court & confessed Judgment for one hundred & forty two Dollars & twenty nine cents, with Interest from the twenty fifth day of Decr 1796, with stay of Execution sixty days, his giving bond with security.

Signed.   Wm Hopkins

Test. N. Willis

Jury N° 2

1. George Hays   7. Dav^d Kilough
2. James Laughridge   8. Ge^o Wallace
3. George Cunningham   9. Saml Pattern
4. Wm Pattern   10. Thos Hightower
5. Nathan Sparks   11. Alex^r Morrison
6. Saml Kilough   12. Jno Wallace

Mathew Finley }
     vs   }
Henry Trent   }

In this case, the Jury Nº 2 were sworn

We, the Jurios, do find for the plaintiff forty ~~four~~ two dollars & [blot] five cents, with cost, without Interest.

Signed.   Jnº Wallace, F. M.

———

X It being represented to this Court that Harriet & Lowness Strickland, being minors & under the years of discretion & children of Henry Strickland, Dec^d, and that it is necessary to have Guardians appointed to take care of the persons & property of the aforesaid minors. Whereupon, it is Ordered, that Mary Strickland, their Mother, be appointed & that letters of guardianship Issue accordingly, She giving bond & security in the sum of two thousand five hundred & 71 dollars for her faithful discharge of that duty.

Mathew Stone }
    vs   }
Jacob Carter   }

In this case, Jury Nº 1 sworn

We, the Jury, find for the Plaintiff Sixty dollars, with cost & Interest.

Signed.   Jnº Wallace, F. M.

Francis Gorden & Cº }
    vs   }
Richd Anderson   }

In this case, Jury Nº 1 sworn

We, the Jury, find for the Plaintiff the Sum of forty two dollars & seventy eight cents, with Interest from the twenty sixth day of Septr 1795, with cost.

Signed.   M. Gathright, F. M.

Appealed.

———

Francis Gorden & Cº }
  vs   }
George Mcfalls }

In this case, the defendant came into Court & confessed Judgment for the sum of sixty four dollars & twenty eight & ¼ cents with interest & cost, Stay of execution six months.

Signed.   George Mcfalls

Test. T. P. Carnes

Francis Gorden & Cº }
  vs   }
Jo^s McCutchin   }

In this case, the def^t came into Court and confessed Judgment for forty one dollars & forty six cents, with Interest from the first day of Jany 1793 & costs. But, this Judgment, as far as the sum of nineteen dollars & twenty eight cents, may be discharged upon producing a voucher for that sum paid to Thos Duke, with the Interest of said sum.

Signed.   Jo^s McCutchin

Jo^s Humphries on the Bench.

Francis Gorden & Cº }
  vs   }
Randolph Traylor }

In this case, the def^t came into Court & confessed Judgment for thirty dolls & fifty two cents, with costs & Stay of Execution six months.

Signed.   Rand^h Traylor

           Joseph Humphries
           James Pittman
           Absalom Ramey

The Court Adj^d till tomorrow 10 o'clock.

B. Easley, Clk

Wednesday, this 3 Jany 1798

The Court met according to adjournment.

Present   Rod^k Easley }
           Ja^s Pittman } Esq^rs
           Abs^m Ramey } on the Bench.

Clary Strickland & Richd Strickland, both of the years of discretion, being children of Henry Strickland, deceased, came into Court and made choice, Clary of his Mother, Mary Strickland, as Guardian, & Richard made choice of Jacob Strickland. Whereupon, it is Ordered by the Court, that Mary Strickland & Jacob Strickland be appointed guardians of the persons & estates of the said Clary & Richard, and that Letters of Guardianship Issue to the said Mary & Jacob, they giving bond & security to the Clk of this Court in the sum of two thousand doll^s each, for the faithful discharge of that trust.

Sq^r Joseph Humphries came in and took his Seat on the Bench, and Rod^k Easley, Esqr retired.

Saml Crowley }
  vs   } Desist
Jordan Anderson }

    In this case, the following Jury were sworn

    1. Jacob Houver   7. Miles Gathright
    2. Jacob Carter   8. Thos Carter
    3. Gallant Runnels   9. Jno McCartney
    4. Martin Gardner   10. George Hays
    5. Jonathan Lane   11. George Cunningham
    6. Wm Jones   12. Wm Pattern

The Jury returned the following Verdict.

We, the Jury, do give the plaintiff, Saml Crowley, twenty seven dollars & 50 Ct^s.

        M. Gathright, F. M.

Wm Strong, Senr, et al }
  vs   } Slander
Saml Knox   }

Cost paid.

In this case, the Plaintiff acknowledged a Non Suit. the Costs paid.

———

Wm Ely }
 vs } Att^t
Ja^s Emet }

   In this case, the following Jury were sworn

  1. Robt Fortenbury   7. Jno Wallace
  2. Nathan Sparks   8. James Armstrong
  3. Saml Kilough   9. Luke Patrick
  4. Alex^r Morison   10. Wm Streatman
  5. Jno Cuningham   11. Danl Mathews
  6. Anderson Watson   12. Buck Ledbetter

the Jury return the following verdict.

We find for the Plaintiff $2142.60, with costs.

Signed.   Jno Cuningham, F. M.

Upon Motion of M. W^{m}son, plantf Att^y, Ordered that the tract of Land which the attach^t was Levied on be sold agreeable to Law.

Ordered, that Tavern Licence be granted Ro^t Fortinberry. Licence Issued.

The Court Adjourned till tomorrow 9 O'clock.

          J. Pittman
          Absalom Ramey
          R^k Easley

B. Easley, Clk

       Thursday, 4 Jany 1798

The Court mett agreeable to adjournment.

        James Pittman }
        Abs^m Ramey   } Esq^{rs}
        Rod^k Easley   }

On the Bench, And made the following orders, to wit.

Ordered, that the Constables now in Office be continued, on their going to the Clerk's Office & giving Bonds agreeable to Law, & that the Clerk notify them of the same.

On Petition of Sundry Inhabitants of this County, praying an order be passed for cutting a Road from Thos Kirkpatrick's Mill shoal on Kurrey's Creek, the nearest & best way to the Cedar Shoal on the Oconee, from thence into a Road cut from Oglethorpe Court house to the County line at or near John George's.

Ordered, the same be cut and David Luckey, Micaj^h W^{m}son, and Absalom Sparks be commissioners to have it Cut from the Cedar Shoal to the County line at or near Jno George's, and Joseph McCutchin, John Nall, and Jno King be commissioners of the other part, from the Cedar Shoal to Killpatrick's Mill Shoal.

A petition of Sundry Inhabitants of the County of Jackson praying a road be cut from Sexton's ford on the Oconee River, the Nearest and most convenient way to the Cherokee Corner.

Ordered, the same be cut, and Benjamin Rice, Arthur Pattern, & Isham Hendon be commissioners to have the same done.

Joseph Humphries, Esqr took his Seat. And retired again.

An Acc^t of D. W. Easley for Stationary amounting to $4.25 was handed in. Ordered, that the same be paid.

Sarah & Elizabeth Blackburn, minors, Daughters of Augustine Blackburn, deceased, came into Court, and Elizabeth made choice of Susan Hardin for her Guardian, & Sarah made choice of Ambrose Cameron for her Guardian. Ordered, that Letters of Guardianship be granted to Susan Hardin & Ambrose Cammeron, on their giving bond & security in two thousand dollars each.

———

It being represented to this Court that Nancy Blackburn, William Blackburn, & Augustine Blackburn, being minors and under the years of discretion and children of Augustine Blackburn, deceased, and that it is necessary to have Guardians appointed to take care of their persons & property of the afores^d minors. Whereupon, it is ordered, that Joseph Humphries, Esqr be appointed and letters of Guardianship be granted, on his giving bond & security in the sum of six thousand dollars for his faithful discharge of the trust.

It being made known to the court that Nancy McCarter, an Orphan child of Jeremiah J. McCarter, between ten and eleven years of age, and not having property sufficient to maintain the orphan. Whereupon, it is ordered, that the said orphan be bound unto ~~Joseph~~ John King, untill she arrives to the age of eighteen, he giving Bond & Security to the Clerk for all necessaries in her education, Clothing, & Victualling.

———

Ordered, that the Clerk do pay unto John Hart that amount of his demand, if he has sufficient funds, the am^t of which is $41.

Josiah Morton, being nominated as a Tax receiver the present year, was appointed, and ordered that he gives Security to the Clerk for the faithfully performance.

Alexander Harper was appointed a Collector of Taxes the present year and ordered that he gives bond for the faithful discharge thereof.

            J. Pittman
            W. Easley
            Absalom Ramey

The Court adjourned untill court in course.

            B. Easley, Clk
            Inferior Court Jackson Ct^y

Saml Crowley }
  vs   } Judgment for $27.50
Jorden Anderson }

The defendant came to the office & gave security for stay of execution Sixty days, himself in the sum of fifty five dollars, & Joshua Hightower in the sum $27.50, this fifth day of Jany 1798.

            Jordan Anderson
            Joshua Hightower

Test. B. Easley, Clk

John Grisham & }
Elizabeth Scott }
  vs   } Judgment for $85
Thos Hightower }
& Joshua Hightower }

Joshua Hightower came to this Office & gave security for stay of Execution sixty days, Joshua Hightower in the Sum of Seven hundred dollars & his security in the sum of fifty dollars.

Acknowledged this 5 Jany 1798.   Joshua Hightower
                  Jordan Anderson

B. Easley, Clk

Francis Gorden & Co }
  vs   }
Richd Anderson }

In this case, there having been Judgment obtained. The defendant came to the Office, paid the cost & appealed.

Benjamin Parr Acknowledged himself Security for the defendant, that is, the defendant shall pay the eventual condemnation money, should there be any, or he will do it for him, or surrender his body to the common Jail of the County, in discharge thereof.

Done at office this 6 day of Jany 1798.   Richard X Anderson, his mark
                  Benjamin Parr

B. Easley, Clk

Licence Issued to Rod^k Easley to Keep Tavern & retail Spirituous Liquors.

Dated the Licence the 2nd Augs^t 1797.

John Smith deposited in the Office eight Dollars in part for Tavern Licence April 4, 1798.

B. Easley, Clk

At an Inferior Court begun & held in and for the County of Jackson the first day of August 1798.

Present, their honors   Rod^k Easley }
,   James Pittman } Esquires
,   Abs^m Ramey }
,   George Wilson }

Francis Gorden & Co }
  vs   } Case
Jacob Carter   }

In this Case, the Defendant came into Court and confessed Judgment, to wit.

I confess Judgment to the plaintiff for Ninety dollars & ten cents, With Stay of Execution Six Months, with Interest from the sixth day of June 1795 & Costs.

Signed.   Jacob Carter

Test. Jn° Griffin

Jury N° 1

1. Ludwell Armstrong	7. Isham Williams
2. Benj^a Rice	8. Charles Gent
3. Anthony Williams	9. Thos Bradshaw
4. Elisha Gentry	10. John Park
5. William Sparks	11. Oliver Laron
6. Absalom Sparks	12. Thos Hych

Robert McAlpin }
  vs   } Atachment
Hugh Calhoon }

In this Case, Stephen Herd, being duly summoned as Guarantee, is sworn in open Court, upon his examination, saeth that he ~~purchased a Still of Calhoon, the def^t, & was to settle it with his Brother, who was to make titles to Calhoon~~, that he has no effects of the defendant in his hands, nor does he owe him one farthing.

Miles Burch & C° }
  vs   }
James & John Parks}

In this case, the Defendants came into Court and confessed Judgment, to wit.

We confess Judgment to the plaintiff for one hundred & eight dollars, with Interest from the third day of June 1795 & Costs & Stay of Execution twelve Months.

Signed.   Jn° Parks
           Ja^s Parks

Test. M. W^{m}son

Andrew McNab }
   vs   }
John Kennerly }

In this Case, the Suit is to proceed in the name of Anne McNab, Extr^x and continued to Next Court.

The Administrators }
of Peter Flemming }
   vs   }
Thos Kennerley }

In this case, John Kennerley came into Court and acknowledged himself special Bail for the defendant, in double the amount mentioned in the bail bond, that is, he shall pay the condemnation

---

Money, he will do it for him, or surrender his body when he is charged in Execution;

Acknowledged in Open Court.   B. Easley, Clk

William Fielder, of the years of discretion and son of William Fielder, Deceased, Came into Court & Made choice of Martin Nalls as Guardian.

Whereupon, it is Ordered by the Court, that Martin Nall be appointed Guardian of the person & estate of said William Fielder, & that Letters of Guardianship issue to the said Martin Nall, he giving Bond & security to the Clerk of this Court in the sum of one thousand Dollars & two Securities in the sum of five Hundred each, for the performance of his duty as Guardian.

The Court adjourned till tomorrow 10 O'clock.

> Rd[k] Easley, JP
> J. Pittman, JP
> Absalom Ramey, JP

Thursday, 2 August 1798

Present, their honors

> James Pittman }
> Rod[k] Easley } Esquires
> Abs[m] Ramey }
> George Wilson }

Edward Phillips }
     vs   } Deceit
Samuel Pattern }

In this case, the following Jury was sworn, to wit

1. Ludwell Armstrong
2. Anthony Williams
3. Elisha Gentry
4. William Sparks
5. Absalom Sparks
6. Isham Williams
7. Charles Gent
8. Oliver Laron
9. Tho[s] Hych
10. William Brand
11. Joseph McCutchin
12. Sam[l] Gardner

Witnesses sworn on

J. N. Cunningham }
G. P. Cunningham }
Andrew Cunningham }
John Barnett } Pltff
Anderson Wilson }
Isaac Midlebroks }
Ch[s] Dougherty }

Jesse Armstrong }
James Armstrong }
[blank] McMullin }
Ja[s] Laughridge } Def[t]

The Jury returned the following Verdict.

We, the Jury, find for the Defendant.

Signed.   Sam¹ Gardner, F. M.

Busby Reynolds }
    vs   }
Miles Gathright }

In this case, Sam¹ Gardner came into Court and acknowledged himself Special Bail, in Double the sum mentioned in the Bail Bond, that is, he shall pay the condemnation money, he will do it for him, or Surrender his body to the common Jail of this County, when he is charged in Execution.

Acknowledged in open Court.

teste. B. Easley, Clk

Uriah Humphries }
    vs   }
George Henry }

In this Case, Thomas Barron Came into Court & acknowledged himself special Bail, that is, he shall pay the condemnation money, he will do it for him, or Surrender his Body to the common Jail of this County, if he is charged in Execution.

test. B. Easley, Clk

[at least two pages missing or not filmed]

---

9. Ordered, that there be a Road laid out & opened from Collonel Easley's Mill on Apalachee to John Melone's Mill, & that Thomas Hills, Roderick Easley, & Isaac Hills be Commissioners for said Road.

10. Ordered, that Gartent Runnels & Alexander Smith be Overseers on the Road leading from Barnet's ferry to the High Shoals on the Appelatche River.

11. Ordered, that Capt Nicholas Tuttle, Jacob Lindsey, & William Parks be Overseers on the Road leading from Clarksboro to Franklin Court House, Or to the County line.

12. Ordered, that the Sum of Six Dollars be paid to Rod^k Easley, As soon as the County have funds for expences on John Linsley.

13. Ordered, that the Tax Collector for the year 1799 pay Capt Samuel Kilough the Sum of twenty Dollars & Eighty Cents, being in full for himself & Company for

———

Guarding William Hodge.

14. Ordered, that the Tax Collector for the year 1799 pay to Thomas Killough the Sum of ten Dollars & fifty Eight Cents, in part for his Services as one of the Guard who Attended William Hodge.

15. Ordered, that James Montgomry be appointed a Justice of the peace in Capt Johnson Clark's Company, in lieu of James Porter, Esquire removed.

16. That William Matthews be appointed a Justice of the peace in Capt Tuttle's Company, in lieu of Thomas Rogers, Esqr deceased.

17. That Isaac Boren & Thomas Hog be appointed Justices of the peace in Capt William Camp's Company.

18. That David Shay be appointed a Justice of the peace in Capt Preston Reynolds District, in lieu of Abner Bankston, Esqr resigned.

———

19. That ~~Capt~~ James McClusky & Saml Henderson be appointed Justices of the peace in Capt William Blake's Company.

20. That Champ^n T. Traylor be appointed a Justice of the peace in Capt Aaron Wood's Company, in lieu of Richd Easley, Esqr, who is turned into a new Company.

21. Ordered, that James Parks, Henry Coone, & Abnor James be Overseers of the Road from Pope's ford on the Oconee, leading in a direction for Gorden's Iron Works in Oglethorpe County.

Signed.   { B. Harriss, J. I. C.
                  { Ja^s Pittman, J. I. C.
                  { Ab^s Ramey, J. I. C.

Test. W. Pentecost, Clk

At An Inferior Court began & held in & for the County of Jackson on the 22nd day of June 1801.

Present, their honors   Bucknor Harriss
,   Absalem Ramey
,   George Willson
,   Micijah Benge, Esquires.

The following Jury Sworn Generally, to wit.

   1. Benjn Watkins   7. Wm Stone
   2. John M'Vay   8. John Moss
   3. Th^o Crane   9. Garret Parks
   4. Randolph Traylor 10. David Luckie
   5. John Hinton   11. Sherwood Horton
   6. Uriah Humphress 12. Bozmon Adare

Wm Strong, Assn^{ee} }
of Danl Head   }
  vs   }
Micajah W^{m}son }

        Jury N° 1, as above

We, the Jury, find for the plaintiff the Sum of three hundred & fifty Dollars, with Lawful Interest & Cost of Suit.

Signed.   Uriah Humphress, f. M.

Jury Nº 2

1. Edm^d Edmonds
2. Joshua Hightower
3. George Ewings
4. Arthur Taylor
5. William Akins
6. Thos Hinton
7. John Thompson
8. Charles Gent
9. Hugh McVay
10. George Haney
11. James Lindsey
12. Prossor Horton

Richd Easley }
    vs   } Slander
John Ware }

Jury Nº 1

We, the Jury, find for the plaintiff five hundred Dollars & Cost of Suit.

Signed.   Uriah Humphress, fm

Richd Easley }
    vs   } False Imprisonment
John Wear }

Jury Nº 2

We, the Jury, find for the Defendant.

Signed.   Ge^o Ewing

The Court Adjourn'd till tomorrow ten O'clock.

Thursday, the 23rd June 1801

The Court Met According to Adjournment, to wit, their Honors

> Bucknor Harriss }
> Absalem Ramey }
> Ja^s Pittman } Esquires
> Micajah Benge }

Saml Little }
    vs   } Deceit
John Kennerley }

Jury N° 1, to wit

1. Ben^j Watkins
2. John McVay
3. Thos Crane
4. John Hinton
5. Wm Stone
6. David Luckie
7. Sherwood Horton
8. Bozman O'dear
9. Uriah Humphress
10. Edwd Edwards
11. Joshua Hightower
12. George Ewing

We, the Jury, find for the Plaintiff fifty Dollars, & Cost of Suit.

Signed.   Wm Stone, f. m.

Jury N° 2, to wit

1. William Akin
2. Thos Hinton
3. John Thompson
4. Chas Gent
5. Hugh McVay
6. Jordain Clark
7. Prosor Horton
8. Arthur Patton
9. Wm Cade
10. Jonathan Lane
11. Wm Strong
12. Thos Colbert

Brooks Mottersherd, Plff }
      vs   }
Talbot Arthur, Claim^t }

Dismist, at the plaintiff's Cost.

Love Stathens }
    vs   } Case
Bedford Brown}

Jury N° 2

We, the Jury, find for the Plaintiff One hundred Dollars & Cost of Suit.

Signed.   Wm Strong, f. M.

———

Nathan Gann }
    vs   } Trover
Arthur Patton }

We, the Arbitrators, award Unto the plaintiff fifty six Dollars, with Cost of Suit.

Signed.   Absalom Ramey
                                  Talbot Arthur
                                  Mica^h Williamson
                                  John Armstrong
                                  Thos Hill
                                  Arbitrators

Nathan Gann }
    vs   } false Imprisonment
Arthur Patton }

We, the Arbitrators, do Award to the plaintiff Ten Dollars, with Cost.

Signed.   Ab Ramey
                                  Talbot Arthur
                                  M. Williamson
                                  Jno Armstrong
                                  Thos Hill
                                  Arbitrators

———

In the two preceeding Cases, the Defend[t] came into Court & entered Security for Stay of execution, when Elisha Wynn Acknowledged himself Bound for the Amount of the two Awards, to wit, Sixty Six Dollars, & Cost of Suit.

Elisha Winn

Test. W. Pentecost, Clk

William Strong }
Ass[ee] of Dan[l] Head }
     vs }
Micajah Williamson }

In this Case, the Defendant Came into Court, paid the Cost which Had Arisen & prayed an appeal, when Richard Easley acknowledged himself Security for the Defendant, to wit, the defendant Shall pay the eventual Condemnation Money, if any, he will do it for him, or Surrender his Body to the Common Jail of Jackson County, when the defendant is Charged in execution.

Rich[d] Easley

Test. W. Pentecost, Clk

Love Stathews }
    vs } Judgment
Bedford Brown }

In the above Case, the defendant Bedford Brown came to the Office, paid the Cost which had Arisen & pray'd an Appeal, when Richard Easley Acknowledged himself Security, that is to say, he the defendant Shall pay the eventual Condemnation Money, if any, he will do it for him, or Surrender his Body to the Common Jail, in discharge of himself, when he the Said Brown, Shall be Charged in Execution.

Rich[d] Easley

Test. W. Pentecost, Clk

Harriss & Carter }
    vs }
Daniel & Rod^k Easley }

By Consent of parties, it is Ordered, that all Matters in dispute be refered to the Arbitrament of Rus Jones & Saml Gardner, Esquires with

―

power of Umpireage, whose Award Shall be return'd to the next term & made the Judgment of the Court, either party giving the Other ten Days Notice of the time of Meeting.

Wednesday, 24th June 1801

The Court Met According Adjournment, to wit,
Bucknor Harriss
Absalom Ramay
James Pittman &
Micaijah Benge, Esquires.

Elisha Wynn }
    vs } Attach^t
John Scutt }

On Motion of Mr Martin, ptff^s Attorney. In this Case, a Horse being Levy'd on, which is of a perishable Nature, it is Ordered, that S^d Horse be sold, in terms of the Act in such Cases made & provided.

John Penington }
    vs }
John Lindsey }

Refer'd.

―

Jury N° 1

1. Sherwood Horton   7. Chas Gent
2. Edmond Edwards   8. Prosor Horton

3. Joshua Hightower
4. Jaˢ Ewing
5. William Akin
6. John Thompson
9. John McVay
10. Jones Henderson
11. Joseph Smith
12. Jacob Lindsey

Appealed by Consent.

Jnº Tweedle }
   vs   } Debt
Jesse Casey }

by leave of the Court, the Interogatories ~~by leave of the Court were Open'd~~ in the above Case were Open'd.

Williamson & Clerk }
   vs   } Attᵗ
George Weatherby }

George Weatherby Came into Court ~~with the~~ & enter'd Special Bail, when Thomas Harriss Acknowledged himself Security, that is to Say, he the Defendant shall pay the eventual Condemnation Money, if any, he

———

Will do it for him, or deliver his, the Defendant's Body, to the Common Jail in discharge of himself, when he shall be charged in execution.

                                          Thoˢ X Harriss, his mark

W. Pentecost

Jnº Tweedle }
   vs   } Debt
Jesse Casey }

In this case, the parties, by consent, entered an appeal to the Superior Court. Interrogatories, on the part of the defendant were Returned Regularly & Afirmed by the counsel for the defendant, with the leave of the Court, & being Well executed, they were Sealed again in Open Court & Ordered to be transmited to the Superior Court & to be Read in evidence, together with all the Other papers appertaining to the above suit.

~~Williamson & Clark~~ }
     vs   }
~~George Weatherby~~ }

Stephen Camp   }
     vs   } Case
Joseph Lemmond }
     &   }
Allen Brazel   }

We, the Jury N° 1, find for the plaintiff the sum of Sixty five dollars, with Interest from the twenty fifth day of December 1799 & cost of suit.

                           Jacob Lindsey, foreman

Jury N° 2, to wit

1. Harmon Reynolds	7. John Adams
2. Thomas Johnson	8. William Caid
3. Brooks Mottersheard	9. Arthur Taylor
4. John McConnell	10. John Ross
5. Walter Bell	11. Ja^s Kirkpatrick
6. Robert Nobles	12. John Kennerly

Joseph Nation   }
     vs   } Case
Thos & Peley Rogers }

We, the Jury N° 2, find for the Plaintiff Ninety seven Dollars & ten cents, with Interest & cost of suit.

                           John McConnell, foreman

Jury N° 1, to wit

1. Sherwood Horton	7. Charles Gentt
2. Edmond Edwards	8. Prosor Horton
3. Joshua Hightower	9. John McVay
4. Ge° Ewing	10. Jones Henderson

5. William Akin
6. John Thompson
11. Joseph Smith
12. Jacob Lindsey

John M. Carter }
  vs   } Case
William Hopkins }

~~We, the Jury Nº 1, find~~

We do find for the plantif forty two Dollars twenty nine cents, with Lawful interest & Cost of suit.

       Ja^c Lindsey, foreman

John Adams }
  vs   }
Jesse Vincent }

In this case, all Matters in Dispute in the above cause are, by consent of parties, Refer'd to the Arbitrament & Determination of Edmond Carlile & James Montgomery, with power of umpirage, their award to be made on or before the first day of next term, & to be Enter'd as the Judgment of this Court.

Alexander }
  vs   } Att^t
Ross   }

       Jury Nº 1

We, the Jury, find for the plantiff fifty Dollars, with cost of suit, with Lawful Interest.

       Ja^c Lindsey, fore^m

Whereas, a Judgment was obtain'd against James Harper, upon a promisory note, given by said Ambrose Camron, for one hundred Dollars, Indorsed to Robert Campbell, & by Campbell Indorsed to William Parks, on which the said Parks recover'd Judgment against said James Harper, & a Capias Ad satisfaciendum Issued, & by the Inferior Court Discharged here under the Insolvent Act.

Whereupon, it is ordered, that the Clerk Deliver up the said Note to the to the said William Parks.

Richard Easley }
     vs   } Slander
John Wear   }

Judgment 500

Costs.

John Wear came to the Office, paid the Cost that had Arisen, & pray'd an Appeal, when John Black Acknowledged himself Security, that is to say, he the Defendant Shall Shall pay the eventual Condemnation Money, if any, he will do it for him, or deliver his Body to the Common Jail of this County, in discharge of himself, when the Defendant shall be charged in Execution.

                                          John Black

W. Pentecost, Clk

Richd Easley   }
     vs   } Case
Richd Thurmond }

                         Jury N° 1

We, the Jury, find for the plaintiff the sum of One hundred & Ninety Six Dollars & fifty Six Cents, & Cost of Suit.

                                      Jacob Lindsey, f. M.

Richd Easley }
     vs   } false Imprisonment
John Wear }

Judg^t for the Defendant.

Richard Easley Came to the Office, paid the Cost which had arisen, & pray'd an Appeal, when David Robertson Acknowledged himself Security, that is to say, he the s^d Easley shall pay the eventual Condemnation Money, if any, he will do it for him, or deliver his Body to the Common Jail of this County, in discharge of himself, when the defendant Shall be Charged in execution.

David P Robertson, his mark

W. Pentecost, Clk

Matthew Knight }
    vs   } Attachment
Thomas George }

Jury N° 2

We, the Jury, find for the plaintiff Sixty four Dollars eighty one & one fourth Cents, with Cost of Suit.

Signed.   J. McConnell, f. m.

The Court Adjourned till the first Monday in August.

                                 B. Harriss
                                 James Pittman
                                 Micajah Benge

At an Inferior Court held in & for the County Jackson, Monday, the 3rd Day of August 1801.

Present, their Honors

                                 Bucknor Harris
                                 James Pitman
                                 Micajah Benge, Esquires.

1. Ordered, that there be a Road open'd & Kept in Repair from the High Shoals of the Apalachee River to the Seat of the University of Georgia, & that Micajah Benge, J. Henry Dixon, & Roger Kagle be Commissioners to lay out & Report on the Said Road.

2. Ordered, that James Rogers be appointed Justice of the peace in Capt Lancaster's District, and that James Nash be appointed a Justice of the peace in Captain Tuttle's District, in the Room of Thomas Rogers, Deceased.

3. Ordered, that Thomas Parks be appointed Overseer of the Road leading from Clarksboro to Mcfall's ford.

4. Whereas, the Commissioners appointed to lay out a Road from the Store of Vann & Davis to Jackson Court house, have Reported to the Court, that have done the Same & Recommended that Joseph Davis, Johnson Clark, Jacob PettyJohn, & Eldridge Hargrave be appointed Overseers of the said Road.

Ordered, that the several Overseers Recommended be appointed in the following Manner, to wit, that Joseph Davis be appointed overseer of that part of said Road lying between [blot] & that all male Tithables [blot] to work on roads [blot]

On the Waters of the pond fork & Allen Creek, above the Junction of said Creeks, to be under him, & Clear the Road from the Store of Van & Davis, to the Crossings the pond fork. That Johnson Clark be Overseer of District N° 2, and all male tithables living on the North Side of the Walnut fork, & the Middle River, & all on the South Side of Curry's Creek, to clear & work on the Road, from the Crossing the pond fork, opposite to John Diamond's, to the branch that Comes from White's Store, Opposite to Thos Kirkpatrick, Esqr. That Jacob PettyJohn be Overseer of Dis^t N° 3. And all male Tithables liable to work on Roads, that live on the North side of the Middle River, as low as George Keeth's, and all on the South Side of Curry's Creek, as low as John Henderson's, to be under him & work on the Road, from the Branch that Comes from White's Store to Red Stone Creek.

Order sent by Robert Montgomery.

That Eldridge Hargrove be Overseer of the Road from the ford of Red Stone Creek to Clarksboro, and all the Hands liable to work on Roads in

& about Clarksboro to be under him, & Clear & Work on the same.

5. Ordered, that a Road be laid out from the Oglethorpe Road near Miles Barnet's, across the Oconee at Hudson's ford, thence to intersect John Barnet's Road, to the High Shoals of the Apalachee, & that John Smith, Thomas Brown, Saml Crawley be the Commissioners to lay the same.

Sent by Capt Strong of Aug^t.

6. Ordered, that George Cathey be appointed Overseer of the Road, in lieu of William Bankston, removed. Also, that Roger Cagle be appointed overseer of the s^d Road, in lieu of Jesse Jenkins, removed.

7. That Nathaniel Deane be appointed overseer of the Road from John Melone's Mill, to Oglethorpe County line, on Direction to Phinizyes.

8. Ordered, that the Road leading from Clarksboro to the Cedar Shoals be open'd agreeable to the Recommendations of James Hill

---

and John Mcfalls, Esqr, & that Martin Nalls & James Hill be appointed Overseers to Open & Keep in Repair the said Road.

9. Ordered, that Daniel Gilaspy be appointed a Constable in Capt Pressley Scurlock's Company.

10. Ordered, that George Stewart be Overseer of the Road leading from Clarksborough to Oglethorpe Court House, from Charles Taylor's to Noketchey Creek, & that the following persons in Capt Killough's Company be liable to work under him on said Road, to wit.

  1. Isaac Killough   16. David Stewart
  2. Ja^s Killough   17. [blank] Mcfeld
  3. Ja^s Green   18. Ja^s Stewart
  4. Arthur Taylor   19. Saml Stewert
  5. Robt Taylor   20. Ge^o Stewart
  6. Chas Taylor   21. Ja^s Stewrt
  7. Isaac Lukie   22. Saml Long
  8. Ambros Camron   23. Th^o Killough
  9. David Williams   24. John Huston
  10. Isaac Hill   25. Elige Jentry
  11. [blank] McCright   26. Elige Jentry

12. John White
13. Allen Killough
14. George Wallis
15. David Wall

27. Jacob Morton
28. Cain Jentry

---

29. Mittenton Ledbetter
30. Th° Rolaleg

31. James Roleghdy

11. Ordered, that John Thurmond & Gartent Runnels be Overseers to Open & Keep in Repair the Road leading from Barnet's ferry to the high Shoals of the Apalachee River. That Absalem Awtrey & William Loyd be Overseers to Keep in repair the Road from the Mouth to Dove's Creek, to where it intersects the Road leading from Barnet's ferry to the High Shoals of the Apalachee River. That John Barnet, Esquire be Overseer from his ferry on the Road leading to the Oglethorpe line.

Sent by Capt Strong.

12. Ordered, that the Road leading from Beach Creek to Kirkpatrick's ford on the Oconee River, do cross Barber's Creek at Paul Williams' ford on s^d Creek, agreeable the report of Gab^l Hubbard & Abner Bankston, Esquires, & that Silas Downs & Benjamin Hagood be overseers of Said Road.

---

13. Ordered, that a Road be laid out begining in Capt Philip's District, where the Road leading from the High Shoals to the Scull Shoals, Crosses the Court house Road, thence by Capt Floyd's thence to Colonel Runnells's, thence the nearest & best way to the Cedar Shoals, on the North fork of the Oconee River. & that Stephen Nobles, Thomas Hill, & William Robertson be Commissioners to lay out the said Road & Report on the same.

15. Ordered, that James Lackey be Overseer of the Road leading from Clarksboro to Oglethorpe Court House, from Creek Nocetchey to the County line, & that the following persons are to work on that part of said Road, to wit.

1. James Wallace
2. Thomas Adams
3. Robt Wallace

12. James Lackey
13. Jesse Scriviner
14. Thomas Simson

4. William Simpson
5. Ludwell Armstrong
6. William Wallace
7. George Taylor
8. Jesse Ostean
9. Olliver Laren
10. Edwd Adams
11. Andrew Com[blot]

15. James Adams
16. John Wakefield
17. James Allen
18. Jacob Faulkenberry
19. Saml Wallace
20. John Wallace
21. Gilbert Simpson
22. William Gray

---

23. Jessee Sparks
24. Arch^d Taylor
25. James Irving
26. John Wallace
27. Jona^n Williams
28. John Faulkenberry
29. Martin Hancock
30. William Kneal
31. Gabriel Loving
32. Rice Simpson
33. Walter Connel
34. James Wallace, Junr
35. Bozmon Adare
36. James Hathorn

37. William Welborn
38. Randolph Traylor
39. Hor^o Walker
40. Isaac Pace
41. James Pace
42. William Pace
43. James Smith
44. William Smith
45. Andrew Miller
46. John Wallace, Junr
47. Benjamin White
48. Danl Pinkston

16. Ordered, that George Scroggins, Jonathan Phair, Joseph Lancaster, & William Deal, be appointed Overseers to open the Road laid out from Clarksborough to the boundary line, Viz^t, George Scroggins to Open Said Road from Clarksborough to Little Cowen's Creek, Jonathan Phair from s^d Creek to the place of Crossing said Creek to John H. Johnson's Road, Joseph Lancaster from said Johnson's Road to the Bridge on the North River, and William Deal from thence to the boundary line, passing by Ree[blot]

---

17. Ordered, that the Clerk do pay Over to Hen^y Miars Nineteen Dollars, being the Valuation of some Cattle, which was sold as Estrays, & since Claim'd by the Indian Tom, who refuses any other satisfaction but the said Cattle, & the Court for the safety of the frontier thinks it best to Adopt this mode.

Paid.

18. Ordered, that Edward Calehan be appointed Overseer of the Road leading from Chandler's Bridge to the ford on big Sandy Creek at Carter's, & that the following familys, or as many thereof as are liable to work on Roads, be subject to work on that part of said Road, to wit.

1. Edwd Callehans
2. John Higgins
3. the Widow Higgins
4. James Miller
5. David McCord
6. William Matthews
7. Jacob Hoover
8. William Carter
9. Charles Strickland
10. Henry Strickland

11. James Holms
12. Henry Stoneham
13. Th^o Rutledge
14. Ben^j Vermillion
15. Joseph Humphrey
16. W Th^o Willingham

---

19. Ordered, that William Robertson be appointed Overseer of the Road leading from Clarksborough to Melon's Mill, & that he Open & Keep in Repair that part of said Road, from John Walls's to the said Mill.

20. Ordered, that the Clerk of this Court Confer with George Matthews on the Subject of Sundry Obligations & Accounts & put them into his Hands for Collection as the property of Jackson County, together with all the documents in his Office relative to County business.

21. Ordered, that Thomas Shannon be discharged from being Overseer of the Road from McColphin's Mill to Jackson Court House, & that Littleton Moss be appointed Overseer of s^d Road in his place.

22. Ordered, that there be a Road laid out from John Shields's Mill, on the pond fork Oconey, the nearest & best way to the Herricane Shoal On

---

the North fork of Oconey, from thence to the Franklin line, where the old trail Crosses, in a line to Maj^r John Holland, & that Robert Venable, Jonathan Phair,

& William Laurence, Esquire be Commissioners to lay out the same & Report thereon.

23. Ordered, that Quinton McCright be Overseer of that part of the Road leading from Clarksborough to Oglethorpe Court House, that lies between the fork of the furniss Road, & ~~Jackson~~ Charles Taylor's, & that the following hands be Subject to work on the same under him, to wit.

1. David Brown
2. Thos Camron
3. John Camron
4. Peter Miller
5. William Brown
6. Levy Tidwell
7. Silas Moote
8. John Hart
9. John Scott
10. Ja^s McWright
11. Johnston Smith

---

24. Ordered, that Robert McCord, Alexander Morrison, & Henry Williams be Overseers to Open & Keep in Repair the Road leading from Pope's ford on the North Oconee River, to a Road leading through Oglethorpe to Augusta, Viz^t, ~~Robt McCord~~ Henry Williams from the County line to little Sandy Creek, Robt McCord, from Pope's ford to Big Sandy, & Alexander Morrison from Big Sandy Creek to little Sandy Creek, & that the hands pointed out by the Commissioners be subject to their Orders in their respective divisions.

By Esqr East.

February Term 1802

At an Inferior Court held in & for the County of Jackson on Monday, the first Day of February 1802, at the place formerly Thomas Kirkpatrick's (But now David Criswell's) in Conformity to the Laws of the last Legislature.

Present, their Honors   Bucknor Harriss   }
                                 James Pittman   } Esquires
                                 William Foster & }
                                 [blank] Hendricks }

51

The following Jury was sworn Generally, to wit

1. John Shields
2. Joseph Kellet
3. John Depriest
4. Richard Turner
5. Michael Moore
6. Zack^h Collins
7. John Moore
8. Ja^s Cuningham
9. John Greene
10. Robert Simpson
11. Nathaniel Hill
12. George Cowen

The Court Adjourned till tomorrow ten O'clock.

Gray & Beal{ "Beal" }   }
    vs   }
Thos & Baley Rogers }

Jury N° 1 sworn Generally

We, the Jury, find for the plaintiff Two hundred & twenty four Dollars & ninety Cents.

H. Montgomery, f. m.

Ordered, that Robert Venable be appointed a Justice of the peace, in the Room of Thomas Kirkpatrick, Resigned.

Ordered, that Eli Towmend be appointed a Justice of the peace, in Said Townsend's District, in lieu of John Diamond, Resigned.

That Robt Johnston be appointed a Justice of the peace in Capt Ja^s Cuningham's Company, in the place of Hugh Montgomery, Esqr, Resigned.

Court adjourned till tomorrow ten o'clock.

Wednesday, the 3rd day of February 1802

The Court met according to adjournment.

Ordered, that Thomas Reynolds be allowed Ninety two Dollars & twenty four Cents for boarding a guard from from the tenth day of December 1801 till the twelfth day of January 1802, & for repairing the Jail ~~Stocks~~ & building Stocks & for boarding guard last Superior Court, to be paid out of the first money belonging to the County unappropriated.

Issued.

Jury N° 1 sworn Generally, to wit

1. Ephraim Lindsay
2. Michael Moore
3. Joseph Kellett
4. John Moore
5. John Green
6. Nathaniel Hill
7. Ge° Cowen
8. James Cunningham
9. Thos Jones
10. Richd Turner
11. Cain Gentry
12. Joseph Humphreys

Joseph Smith & }
Brook Mothershed } Case
    vs }
John Woods }

Jury as above

We, the Jury, find for the plaintiff the Sum of forty four Dollars & [blot] one & a quarter Cents & Cost of Suit.

John Green, f. M.

Feby the 2nd 1802

The Court met agreeable to adjournment.

Jury N° 1 Sworn generally, to wit

1. Ephraim Lindsay
2. Michael Moore
3. Joseph Killett
4. Richard Turner
7. John Green
8. Nathaniel Hill
9. George Cowan
10. James Cunningham

    5. Zachariah Collins   11. Thos Jones
    6. John Moore   12. Hugh Montgomery

Samuel Nelson   }
    vs   } Case
Th^o Kirkpatrick   }

                Jury N° 1 as above

We, the Jury, find for the Defend^t.

                          H. Montgomery, F. M.

Ordered, that Arthur Foster be appointed a Justice of the peace in Capt Scurlock's Company, in room of William Foster, Esqr, appointed a Justice of the Inferior Court.

                          B. Harriss, J. I. C.
                          Ja^s Pittman, J. I. C.
                          Jno Hendricks, J. I. C.

Ordered, that Jacob Lindsay do, in conformity to his obligation, pay over to Judith Peck the sum of twenty Dollars, which was considered by the Court as a reasonable sum for her Expences for her lying in with a bastard child &c &c.

Ordered, that Isaac Hill be appointed Overseer of the Road leading from Clarksborough to Van's Store, on that part that Johnston Clark was Overseer on, & the same hands to work under him that work^d under said Clark.

Elliot Hodge   }
    vs   }
Robert Montgomery }

                      Jury N° 1

We, the Jury, find for the plaintiff Eighty five Dollars Seventy one Cents, with Interest from the time it became due & Cost of Suit.

                          H. Montgomery, fm

Etheldred Wood }
    vs   }
John Pritchett }

Jury N° 1

We, the Jury, find for the plaintiff one hundred & twenty dollars, with Interest from the time the Notes became due & Cost of Suit.

H. Montgomery, fm

Edmund Penn }
    vs   } Trover
Wm Robinson }

On Motion of Plaintiff's Counsel.

It is ordered, that the Clerk transmit the proceedings of this case to the Clerk of the Inferior Court of Clarke County, the place of Residence of the Defendant.

Harris & Carter }
    vs   }
Rod^k Easley & }
Daniel W. Easley }

We, having been appointed by the Honorable the Inferior Court in June Term Eighteen hundred & one as Arbitrators to determine & finally Settle all disputes & controversys between the said copartners, & having heard all the parties, & finding them not to disagree as to facts. We, the said Arbitrators, whose names are hereunto Subscribed, taking upon us the award, and having fully examined the books of the copartners kept, do for the settling, amity, & friendship between the said parties make & declare this our Award by & between the said parties, in manner following, that is to say. We do award & Order that Rodrick & W. Easley shall pay to Buckner Harris & John M. Carter seventeen hundred & Eighty Seven Dollars Nineteen & a half Cents, which appears by the books of the firm Justly due the said Harris & Carter & [faint] two hundred dollars less than what appeared by the Shewing of the parties, but giving up by the parties on the Suggestion of the Defense, which was Stated to be a Dividend less sustained in their dealings. Witness our hands at Clarksborough this 3 day of October 1801.

Levi Gardner
Russel Jones

William Stith   }
      vs   }
Orsbourn Brewer }

Jury N° 2 as above

We, the Jury, find for the Plaintiff Sixty Dollars, with Interest & Cost of Suit.

Green, FM

Ordered, that the Tax collector pay unto Robert Lynch $8.75, James J. McMullin 4.50, & Andrew Jeter .50, amounting on the whole to 28 $ & 50 Cents. It being an allowance made to them for guarding a Criminal (Hodge), who was Executed in the County of Jackson. To be paid by the Tax collector out of the first money that comes into his hands belonging to the County.

Feby Term 1802

James Dubose   }
     vs   }
Dempsey Rogers }

Settled.

Ordered, that the Sheriff of this County do proced to have the Jail of said County put in good repair with sufficient locks &c and that he do take on the [faint] in his hands belonging to the County to defray the said Expences.

[at least two pages apparently missing]

---

10 Ordered, that the Justices of the several districts in Jackson County do report to the next Inferior Court for said county the names of all persons retailing Spirituous Liquors Without Licence, ~~and that the Clerk~~ notify them by Having an order serv^d.

Jury N° 2 To wit

1. Alexander McDonald
2. Elisha Winn
3. Joseph Smith
4. Jordain Clark
5. Thomas Townsend
6. Eldridge Hargrove
7. Stephen Jackson
8. Joseph McCutchin
9. William Potts
10. Proser Horton
11. Levy Townsend
12. Joseph Laymaster

Saml Gardner, ass^{ee} }
    vs }
John Armour & }
Wm Cain }

Jury N° 2

We, the Jury, find for the Plaintiff Seventy five Dollars, with Interest & Cost.

John Greene fm

~~William Milton~~ }
    vs }
~~Bartley Wooten &~~ }
~~Gilley Wooten~~ }

~~Jury N° 2~~

~~We, the Jury, find for the Plaintiff two hundred Dollars, with Interest & Cost of Suit.~~

Matt Knight }
    vs }
John L. Sherman }

Jury N° 2

We, the Jury, find for the Plaintiff forty one Dollars Ninety Seven Cents, with Cost of Suit.

John Green, f m

Hall & Cosby }
    vs   }
McFalls   }

Jury N° 1 as formerly, Except John Green, In his place Joseph Laymaster

We, the Jury, Consider the property Subject to Execution.

Joseph Laymaster, fm^n

Gray & Beal   }
    vs   }
Thos & Peley Rogers }

Judgm^t for two hundred & twenty four Dollars & Ninety Cents & Cost of Suit.

In this Case, Peley Rogers, one of the Defendants, Came into Court & Stay of Execution, James Rogers Expressing himself Security for the Same.

Peley Rogers

Acknowledged in open Court.   Ja^s Rogers

W. Pentecost, Clk

Ordered, that the Tax Collector for Jackson County pay to Abraham & Joseph Lindsay the Sum of one hundred Dollars out of the tax levyed for Building a Bridge.

Ordered, that Obadiah Light pay to Elizabeth Hendricks the Sum of Twenty Dollars for the Expences of her Lying in & attendance when she had her Bastard Child, Otherwise his Obligation will be tried.

3rd Feby 1802

On Motion of Council for [faint] it is Ordered, that the Clerk [faint] Court of Jackson County [faint] Statement of the [faint] the defendants reside [faint] the Clerk of the Inferior [faint] upon those making the [faint] the Costs that has Accrued [faint] to wit.

> N° 3 of June Term [faint]
> Crawford [faint]
> N° 15 June Term 1801
> N° 20 June Term 1801
> N° 28 June Term 1801
> N° 2 of February Term 1802

> N° 7 of February Term 1802
> N° 14 of June Term 1801

Ordered, that John Vanable, Jonathan Cook, Owen ~~Thomas~~ Shannon, & William Kellett be appointed Overseers of the Road leading from Shields's Mills, on the [faint] fork of the Oconee, to the Herricane Shoal, & from thence to the Franklin line, to wit. John Venable from said Mills to Maj^r Criswell's Mill, Jonathan Cook from said Criswell's Mill to the South fork of Parker's Creek, & Owen Shannon from said South fork to the Herricane Shoal, & William Kellet from the said Herricane Shoal to franklin.

Ordered, that there be a Road lay'd out [faint] Candler's Creek & North fork of Oconee, Crossing Said Creek at [faint]

[faint] Miller, Nathan [blot] Finch, Joseph Smith, Isaac [faint], Benjamin Browning, James Bogs, Mr Rutledge, Ezekiel Bowman, Isaac Ivy.

Ordered, that Leon Pritchett be & he is hereby appointed Overseer of the road leading from Bearden's Bridge on the North Oconee to John Casey's on the Franklin line, & that he be vested with full power to alter & mend said Road any way as not to affect any persons' premises, that the said Alterations be a nearer & better way than the present Road.

Issued.

Ordered, that Leon Pritchett be & he is hereby appointed an Over to open & Keep in Repair the road leading from Diamond Hill to Bearden's Bridge, & the following hands to work under him, John Hamilton, Junr, William Watkins, W^m M[blot],

———

Wm Casey, Thomas Holland, William McCorkle, & all within their bounds that are liable to work on Roads.

Issued.

Ordered, that John Carmichael be & he is hereby appointed overseer of the Road from Bearden's bridge to Crawford's on the pond fork, & the following hands to work on said Road, to wit. Wm Dickson, Wm Blake, Middleton Brooks, Wm Boyd, Senr, Peter Lankford, Robert Lankford, & all within their bounds that are liable to work on Roads.

Issued.

Ordered, that Samuel Coasey be & he is hereby appointed Overseer of the Road from the Pond fork to John McConnis's, Junr, & the following hands to work on said Road, to wit. Mark Doss, Obadiah Light,

———

Alexander Cowen, Robert Montgomery, & all within said bounds that are liable to work on Roads.

Issued.

Ordered, that Samuel Wilson & Edmund Grisham be Overseers of the Road from John McElhannon's bridge to intersect a Road leading from Jefferson to Athens, as laid Out by Samuel Wilson & John Muckelhannon, the following hands do work under them Catchens Martin, McElhannon, Shields, Camp, John Martin, Lowry, Samuel Wilson, Green Wood, Hewety Brown, Hobson, McDermont, Gardner, Wright, John Ross, Wiley Ross, Wm Miller, Rasberry Finch, Edwards, House, Barnett, Ebenezer Miller, Charles Miller.

Issued.

[blot] }
    vs   } Judgm^t on Att^a
Jonathan Pharr }

On Motion of counsel for plaintiff, stating that Edward Pharr, who was summoned as a Garnishee in the above case, has returned as the property of the said Jonathan several grants & Deeds for lands & other papers evidences of debt. It is Ordered, that the Sheriff sell the lands not in possession of any other person, after duly advertising, & pay the proceeds thereof into the Clerk's office, & that the plaintiff have the liberty of suing for any lands for which the Documents of title have been returned by the said Edward, & which lands are in the possession of any other person, & when recovered be in like manner sold by the Sheriff as aforesaid, & the proceeds thereof paid into the Clerk's Office, & to be subject to the further order of this Court. That the plaintiff have also the liberty of suing any of the said evidences of Debt which he shall deem recoverable, to be in like manner when recovered paid into the Clerk's Office.

Wednesday, 29 Jany 1800

The Court met agreeable to Adjournment.

Present   B. Harris }
                                    Ja^s Pittman } Esquires
                                    A. Ramey }
                                    M. W^{m}son }

Ordered, that John Wallace be appointed a Justice of Peace for the County of Jackson in Capt Traylor's Company, in the place of Paul Patrick, Esqr, remov'd.

That John Mayo be appointed a Justice of the Peace in Capt Joseph Reynolds' District, in place of Samuel Gardner, resigned.

That James Thurmond be appointed a Justice of the Peace in Capt Tuttle's District, in room of Wm Carter, removed.

That Richard Easley be appointed a Justice of the Peace in Capt Aron Wood's District, in room of Wm Pentecost, resigned.

Also, Johnson Strong be appointed a Justice of the Peace in Capt Preston Runnels' District.

———

Ordered, That William Daniel, Junr, Collector of Taxes, pay to Moses Landrith, a pauper, twenty Dollars out of the ~~Money~~ Taxes Levied for the benefit of the poor.

Ordered, That James Britain be exempt from paying a poll Tax & public Duty, by reason of old age & infirmity.

Ordered, That Ch^s Dougherty, Chatt. D. Scroggins, & Talbot Arthur be Overseers to open a Road from the Cedar Shoal on Oconee to the Cherokee Corner. And, that all persons Within two Miles of said road be Obliged to work on it, unless they work on a neared Road.

Ordered, That a Road be Opened from Daniel Bankston's Mill until is shall intersect with McAlpin's Road leading to Clarksborough, & that Henry Trent, Peter Hagler, & James Britain be Overseers, & that all persons living in two miles thereof be obliged to work on said road, unless they work on some neared road.

Ordered, That Maj^r John Wallace, Maj^r Ge^o Taylor, & Thos Scrivener be commissioners to lay out a road from Clarksborough to Lexington near Norris's.

———

Ch^s Rick   }
    vs   } Judgment
Robt Campbell }

In this case, Robert Campbell came to the Office, paid the Costs that had arrisen, & prayed an appeal. Jett Thomas acknowledged himself security, that is, the Defendant shall pay the eventual condemnation money, should there be any, he will do it for him, or surrender the defendant to the Common Jail of the County, in discharge of himself, when the defendant is charged in Execution.

Robert Campbell
Jett Thomas

Teste. B. Easley, Clk

Jethro Mobley }
    vs   }
Wm Watkins }

Eleazer Mobley }
    vs   }
William Watkins }

In these two cases, the Defendant came to the Office with his friend, Ge° Harper, who Acknowledged himself Security for the Defd^t for Stay of Execution 60 days.

W^m + Wadkins, his mark
Ge° Harper

Ordered, That a Road be laid out from Clarksborough to the Head of the Mulberry Fork of Oconee on County line. That John Shields, John Ross, & John McIver be Commissioners to open & Keep in repair the said road & that all persons living in two miles of said shall be Obliged to work on it except they work on some nearer road.

Ordered, That a Road be laid out from Clarksborough to Hugh Montgomery's, & that Hugh Montgomery, James Montgomery, & John Chapman be the Commissioners.

Ordered, That Robert McCord, John Espy, esq^r be appointed Overseers of the road from Pope's Ford on the North Oconee to the Sulpher Springs, & that all persons within two miles be obliged to work on said road.

Ordered, That the Clerk do Issue Tavern Licence until Court in Course to such as apply & comply with the Law.

(Signed)   B. Harris
                            Ja^s Pittman
                            A^b Ramey

Test. B. Easley, Clk

___

Phillip Wray, Ind^{ee} }
    vs   } Judgment
John Hansel   }

In this Case, John Hansel & Thos Benton came to the Office & acknowledged themselves bound to the plaintiff in Double the sum mentioned in the Judgment for stay of execution Sixty days in conformity to the Laws in such cases made & provided.

Feby 1 1800

Signed.   John H Hansel, his mark
                            Thos ∞ Benton, his mark

Teste. B. Easley, Clk

Court Adjourned 'till the 15th Feby next.

                            M. Williams, J. P.
                            B. Harris, J. P.
                            A. Ramey, J. P.

Feby 15 1800, the Court met according to Adjournment, to wit.

                            Bucknor Harris }
                            M. Williams & } Judges
                            A. Ramey   }

Ordered, that the Clerk give to Mr Jett Thomas Notes & Other Obligations due the

___

Inferior Court for the Sale of Publick Lotts to the Am^t of four Hundred Dollars, being in consideration of his undertaking to build & Compleat a Jail for the County of Jackson, from which several demands is for the use of s^d ~~County~~ Thomas.

Ordered, that Swan Harden be Appointed Guardian to Wm Blackburn & Augustin Blackburn, Junr, & that Rod^k Easley be taken as Security.

B. Harris, J. P.
A. Ramey, J. P.
M. Williamson, J. P.

Court Adjourn'd to the 22nd March.

June the 7th 1800

The following Jury Drawn in the presence of Bucknor Harris & Micajah Williamson, Esquires, to wit.

1. John Townsend
2. Thos Burk
3. Harris Tiner
4. Obediah Light
5. William Briant
6. John Saveall
7. Robert Burk
8. Jessee Cain
9. Allen Killough
10. Benjn Freeman
11. Ja^s Park
12. Ephraim Fulgen
13. Robt Willson
14. Jno Wallace, Senr
15. Chas Taylor
16. Lewis Pyron
17. William Black
18. Thos Bradshaw
19. Danl Matthews
20. Thos Johnson
26. Arthur Bearden
27. Joseph Shields
28. Bartlet Wooten
29. Joseph Morton
30. John Biggerstaff
31. Thos Hopper
32. Wm Williamson
33. Joseph Wallace
34. Wm Gentry
35. John Wallace, Junr
36. Wm Hannah
37. Jerem^h Elsberry
38. John Templeton
39. Robert Diamond
40. Jno Watkins
41. Ja^s Hendricks
42. Parks Chandler
43. John Bailey
44. Stephen Morgan
45. Sewil Holland

21. John Horton
22. Jeremiah Holliday
23. William Deal
24. John Barnet
25. John Eastice

46. Bonner Compton
47. Sol⁰ Strickland
48. Ja^s Bankston

Test. W. Pentecost, Clk

June Term 1800

At an inferior Court began & held in & for the County of Jackson on the fourth Monday in June 1800.

Present, their Honours
,
,

Buc^r Harris }
M. Williamson } Esquires
G. Willson }

Jury N⁰ 1 Sworn Generally, to wit

1. Thos Burk
2. Allen Kilough
3. Ben Freeman
4. Jn⁰ Wallace
5. Ch^s Taylor
6. Lewis Peron

7. Sol^n Strickland
8. Wm Deal
9. Jo^s Shields
10. Josiah Mortin
11. Henry Townsend
12. Parks Chandler

John Branham }
    vs   }
Ge⁰ Mcfalls, et al }

Jury N⁰ 1

We, the Jury, find for the Plaintiff four hundred & fifty Dollars, with Cost of Suit.

Josiah Morton, fm

Jury Nº 2 Sworn generally, to wit

1. ~~Thoˢ~~

1. Wᵐ Williamson
2. Wᵐ Gentry
3. John Wallace
4. Jaˢ Parks
5. Barthoʷ Wallace
6. Wᵐ Ramey
7. Thoˢ Kirkpatrick
8. Robᵗ McGowin
9. Patrick Shields
10. Samˡ Henderson
11. Geº Wallace
12. Thoˢ Shields

Wᵐ Strong, Assᵉᵉ }
    vs   }
M. Williamson }

In this case, the note of hand, on which the action is founded, was produced as evidence, when the council for the Defendant objected on the ground ~~of~~ that the words, or Order or Bearer were omitted and the Note not negotiable, on argument, the Court sustain'd the motion upon which the council for the plaintiff excepts to the Opinion of the Court as being contrary to Law.

                            Walton, Plaff council

Bucknor Harris }
    vs   } Attᵗ
Jaˢ Calahan & }
Jacob Forsythe }

We, the Jury, find for the plaintiff five hundred Dollars, with Interest & Cost.

                            J. Morton, f. m.

Elias Alexander }
    vs   } Attachment
John Ross   }

In this case, ~~the defendant~~, Jnº Diamond came into Court & enter'd himself Special Bail for the Defendant ~~in this case~~, that is, that the party Defendant shall pay the Money Awarded, that they will do it for him, or Render up the defendant in discharge of himself, when he the defend^t is charged in execution.

John Diamond

W. Pentecost

Court adjourned till Tuesday 10 O'clock.

M. Williamson, J. P.
Ge^o Wilson
B. Harris

Tuesday, June the 24th 1800, the Court met according to adjournment, to wit.

George Willson }
A^b Ramey & }
Ja^s Pitman }
Esquires }

Micajah W^{m}son }
    vs   } Attachm^t
Wm Few }

The defendant, being 3 times Solemly called & not answering, it is Consider'd by the Court that Judgm^t be entered by default.

---

1. Order'd, that the Clerk, on application, grant Tavern Licence in terms of the Act.

2. Order'd, that James Huie & George Reid be and they are hereby appointed Justices of the peace in District N° 15 in Capt James Cockran's Company.

3. Ordered, that Gabriel Hubbard, Jacob Bankston, James Stringer, Robt McGowin, Richd Easley, Wm Loyd, Richd Thurmond be Commissioners to & lay out a Road leading from the high Shoals of the Apalachee to Jackson Court House, so as to Cross the bridge a Cross the Middle River, where the County may appoint.

4. Order'd, that a Road be laid out, begining at or near Harmon Runnels's, thence leading down across the waters of Roe's Creek to the Greene County line, to Join a Road leading to the Skull Shoals, & that Will Burford & Phillip Tegnor be appointed Surveyors to lay out the same.

5. Ordered, that a Road be laid out from William Foster's on the Apalachee to the Skull Shoals, and Another from the same place to the Jackson Court House, &

---

that John Woods, George Foster, & Mark McClendon be Commissioners to lay out the same & report thereon.

6. Ordered, that the Clerk do pay to Jett Thomas all the money which now is, or may hereafter, come into his Hands for the use of the County, & Subject to the Order of this Court, & which have been heretofore appropriated, untill the Demand of the said Thomas be satisfied for building the Jail of this County, for which he was to have Seven hundred & Ninety Seven Dollars. And, that the Clerk deliver up the Several Obligations due for Lotts sold by this Court to George Matthews, Esqr, Attorney at Law, & that as soon as the Money is recover'd, it be apply'd to the use of discharging the ballence that may be then due to the said Thomas, & that he be allowed lawful Interest on his said demand from the first day of Jany last (1800).

7. Ordered, that William ~~Skurlock~~ Foster & Presley Skurlock be appointed Justices of the Peace for District N° 17 in Capt Joshua Skurlock's Company. That Wm Laurence & James Hendricks be appointed Justices for District N° 16 in Capt Hendrick's Company. That John Martin Carter be appointed a Justice of the peace in Capt Thomas Runnels' district, in the place of Rod^k Easley,

---

Esquire resigned. That Col° Rod^k Easley be appointed a Justice of the Peace to fill a vacancy in Capt Hopkins' District N° 9.

8. Ordered, that William Pounds, an infirm person, be exempted from paying Poll tax.

9. Ordered, that a Road be laid out from the ~~dividing~~ Boundery line to Clarksborough, begining on the dividing ridge between the North fork of the Oconee River & Candler's Creek to deal's ~~Mill~~ Bridge on the said River, & from

thence the most convenient & best way to the said place, & that Benjn Watkins, Jo^s McCutchins, & William Potts be qualified to lay out the same & report thereon.

10. Whereas, it is considered by the Court, that it would be of the utmost Utility to the Inhabitants of this County to erect two Publick Bridges in said County, to wit, one across the North fork of the Oconee at or near the Cedar Shoals, and the other at or near the head of the Long Shoals of the middle fork of the said Oconee River, and that the

---

Tax Collector for said County levy & Collect a tax equal to one Sixth of the Original tax, for the purpose of building & Keeping in repair the said Bridges, & that Daniel W. Easley & William Melone be the commissioners to superintend the leting & building the Bridge at the Cedar Shoals, and that Robt McGowin & Richard Easley be the Commissioners to superintend the letting & building the Bridge near the head of the long Shoals on the Middle fork of the said Oconee River, & that the Clerk serve the Commissioners with a Copy of this Order.

11. The Court having received information that Sarah Watson, a person in a State of Insanity, & as it hath also been said that she has property in the hands of Joseph Humphress, Esqr, we therefore have thought proper to Appoint Benjn Vermillion as a Guardian, to act for her, under the direction of this Court, & that he do report specially every Six Months.

---

12. Ordered, the Tax Collector levy & Collect a Sum equal to one fifteenth of the General Tax, for the benefit of the Poor, & pay it into the Hands of Thomas Hill, Overseer of the poor for Jackson County, & that the Clerk serve the Collector with a Copy of this Order.

John Branum }
    vs   } ~~Judgment~~ Appeal
Ge^o Mcfalls, et al }

In this case, the defendants came to the Office, paid the Cost that had arisen, and pray'd an Appeal, when John Black & Humphrey Scroggin acknowledged themselves Security, that is, they the defendants Shall pay the eventual Condemnation Money, if any, they will do it for them, or deliver their Bodies to the Common Jail of the County, in discharge of themselves, when they the defendants Shall be Charged in execution.

Jnº Black
Humphrey Scroggin

W. Pentecost, Clk
25 June 1800

The Court Adjourned Untill the Second Monday in July for County business.

July 14, 1800, the following Jury Drawn in Presence of James Pitman & Micajah W^{m}son, Esquires, to wit.

1. John Depriest	11. Ben Anderson
2. James Glenn	12. George Butler
3. Saml Niblack	13. Absalom Tidwell
4. Newmon Pounds	14. Jailes Thomas
5. John Dimond	15. Wm Curnton
6. Ed^d Williams, Senr	16. Wm Potts
7. Jnº Hansel	17. Ja^s Armstrong, J^r
8. Elex^r Harper	18. James Thurmond
9. Elex Maharge	19. Jnº Fielder
10. Allen Braswell	20. Jnº Worthen
	21. Abed Moore
	22. Matt Wood

---

23. James Geddian	30. Wm Kirkland
24. Wm Raney	31. Jnº Townsinds
25. Talbert Arthur	32. Abnor James
26. Saml Barnet	33. Ezek^l B. Park
27. Jnº Ross	34. Jnº Bradshaw
28. Wm Scott	35. Benjn Watkins
29. Wm Smith	36. Andrew Miller

January Term 1801

[blank page]

On the first Monday in January 1801 (being the 5th Day of s^{d} Month) being the Day appointed by the Legislature to Elect a Receiver of Tax Returns & Collector of Taxes for the ~~year~~ present year.

Present, their Honors   Bucknor Harris
                                      Micaijah Benge

Judges of the Infer^{r} Court &

Johnson Strong, Peter Colb, Gab^{l} Hubbard, Jno Martin Carter, Richd Easley, & Eth^{d} Wood, Justices of the peace. When the Ballotts were Counted, it appeared that Eth^{d} Wood was Elected Collector & Jacob Bankston Receiver of Tax Returns.

January Term 1801

At an Inferior Court began & held in & for the County of Jackson, on Monday the 26th January 1801, present their Honors

,   Bucknor Harriss }
                                 George Willson & } Esquires
                                 Micajah Benge   }

The Sheriffs return'd the following panel, to wit.

N° 1

1. John Depriest
2. James Greene
3. Alexander Mehargue
4. William Curnton
5. Abednego Moore
6. Talbert Arthur
7. Matt Wood

8. John Ross
9. John Bradshaw
10. Andrew Miller
11. Saml Killough
12. Luke Durbin

Sworn Generally.

John Lucky }
    vs   } Debt
Thos Townsend}

Jury N° 1

We, the Jury, find for the Defendant.

Signed.   Talbot Arthur, f. M.

~~Ordered that~~ On application of Mr Griffin, in favour of John Truman, Jailer of Hancock County, for for the expences of the Unfortunate Hodge, Amounting to Seventy two Dollars Eighty seven & a half Cents, agreeable to an order of Court of the third of August 1799. Ordered, that William Potts, Esqr, Collector of Taxes for Jackson County for the year 1800, do pay over to John Griffin, Esqr the Said Sum of Seventy two Dollars Eighty Seven & a half Cents, out of any Moneys which he may have in hand belonging to the said County.

                                    B. Harris, J. I. C.
                                    George Wilson, J. I. C.
                                    Micajah Benge

The Court adjourned untill tomorrow 10 O'clock.

The Court met agreeable to adjournment, on the bench their honors

                                    B. Harris
                                    A. Ramey &
                                    James Pittman, Esquires.

The following Jury sworn generally, to wit

1. ~~Jnᵉ Depriest~~ Martin Nall
2. Wᵐ Curnton
3. Abednego Moore
4. Mathew Wood
5. Jnᵒ Ross
6. Uriah Humphries
7. ~~Robᵗ McGowin~~ Jnᵒ Bradshaw
8. Jnᵒ Green
9. Peter Buckels
10. Abner Bankston
11. Walter Bell
12. Wᵐ Park

Isaac Penington }
    vs   }
Robᵗ Willson & }
Elijah Hendon }

Jury Nᵒ 1

We, the Jury, find for the plaintiff One hundred & forty two Dollars & Eighty three Cents, & Costs.

Signed.   M. Nall, f. m.

Jeffery Easley }
    vs   }
Joseph Simons }

I confess Judgment in this case for sixty eight Dollars & fifty Cents & cost, with stay of Execution six months, with cost.

                           John Griffin, Attᵒ for Dⁿᵈᵗ

1. Order'd, that Majʳ Joseph Carson be Authorized to furnish two Indian Women, who lies Wounded in his Neighbourhood, with Such Necessaries as he may deem proper for their Support, & that he

furnish the Doctor, & Attendance with Provisions, & that the Clerk be authorized to pay to the amount of twenty five Dollars.

        B. Harris, J. I. C.
        J. Pittman, J. I. C.
        Absalom Ramey, J. I. C.

Wm Green &   }
B. J. Dowdle   }
  vs   } Debt
Jonathan Nobles }

We, the Jury, find for the plaintiff Eighty five Dollars & Sixty Eight Cents.

        M. Nall, F. M.

Jany 26th 1801. We, the under written, being appointed Arbitrators to settle a certain controversy between Robert Campbell & the executors of the Estate of Anthony Ollive, dec^d, did meet agreeable of the Order of Court on that Case, & did make an award in Writing, & returned it to the Clerk, & it appears to have been lost or mislaid, that it cannot be found, now we, the under written, do certify the award to be as follows. The said Robert Campbell shall make or cause to be made warrantable & Sufficient Titles to two hundred & thirty Acres of

---

[blot] George Whitsell, & the Survey that James Knox lives on, & further to pay Seventy Dollars in Cost, on or before the last day of the next term, from which the order was made out.

Certified by us.   Saml Gardner
           Ja^s Pittman
Signed.   Jno Hampton
           Isaac Hill
           Th^o Johnson

Entered, by order of Court in Term.

Test. W. Pentecost, Clk

        Jury N° 1

~~1. James Elam~~
~~2. Alexand^r McHard~~
~~3. Andrew Miller~~

Th^o Morriss & }
Ruth Morriss }
formerly Ruth Oneal }
      vs } Coven^t
Stephen & Cader Powell }

We, the Jury, find for the plaintiff Sixty Dollars & Eighty five Cents.

                         M. Nall, F. M.

             Jury N° 2 Sworn generally, to wit

1. James Glen	7. Richd Easley
2. Alexander Mchard	8. John Waller
3. Andrew Miller	9. Garret Parks
4. Talbert Arthur	10. George Wallace
5. John Dimond	11. John Nall
6. James Hill	12. James Scott

Witt & Cosby }
     vs }
David McNeely }

                     ~~Jury N° 1~~

Settle^d at the Defendant's Cost.

Robt Ellisson }
     vs }
H. Scroggins & }
Th^o Scroggins }

Settled at the Defendant's Cost.

Nathaniel Hill }
    vs }
John Townsend }

Jury N° 2

We, the Jurors, find for the plaintiff two hundred Dollars.

Richd Easley, F. M.

Eli Eavenson }
    vs }
John Depriest }

Jury N° 1

We, the Jury, find for the plaintiff forty four Dollars & Seventy five Cents, with Cost of Suit.

M. Nall, F. M.

Witt & Cosby }
    vs }
Ge° McFall }

Judgm^t confess^d.

J. Jewel }
    vs }
Jn° Melone & }
Wm Roberson }

Judgm^t confess^d.

Ordered, that Mr George Philips be appointed Guardian to Tempy Strong & Jemima Strong, Minors of Elijah Strong, dec^d, & that Lewis Pope be Security.

John Griffin, for }
the use of Harper }
  vs   }
Matthew Wood }

Judgm^t confess^d for forty five Dollars & Ninety five Cents, & Costs, & Stay of Execution Six Months.

Sign^d.   Matt Wood

———

     Jury N° 2, except John Diamond & his place Jethro Mobly

David Witt, Assignee }
  vs   }
William Hamilton }

Settled at the Defend^{ts} Cost.

James Findley }
  vs   }
Saml Gardner }

       Jury N° 1

We, the Jury, find for the Defendant.

          Martin Nall, F. M.

Wm Gough }
  vs   }
James Stringer }

Jury N° 2

We, the Jury, find for the Plaintiff Six hundred Dollars.

R. Easley, f. m.

B. Harris, J. I. C^t
Ja^s Pittman
Absolom Ramey

Court adjourned till Tomorrow 10 O'clock.

Wednesday, 28th Jany 1801

Court met agreeable to Adjournment.

Jury N° 1 Sworn Generally, to Wit

1. Martin Nall
2. William Curington
3. John Ross
4. Abednego Moore
5. Alexander Mchead
6. Talbert Arther
7. Uriah Humphres
8. Richard Easley
9. Walter Bell
10. John Nall
11. William Ramey
12. George Kennedy

Brooks Mottersherd, Ass^{ee} }
    vs }
John Parks }

We, the Jury, find for the plaintiff forty six Dollars & thirty two & a half Cents.

M. Nall, F. M.

Jury N° 2 Sworn, to wit

1. Joseph Lane
2. Joseph Clarkson
3. Thomas Hych
4. Henry McCoy
7. William Strong
8. William Robertson
9. Benjn Rice
10. Burket Dean

5. James Armstrong   11. Thomas Kirkpatrick
6. Edmund Edwards   12. Robert McGown

[the following page not in chronological order]

At Chambers, 24th Sept' 1800

William Strong, Ass^ee }
of Daniel Head   }
     vs   }
Micajah Williamson   }

Exceptions taken to Judgment of the Inferior Court, & by consent of parties, now argued before the Superior Court on the Exceptions in Writing, & now filed with the Clerk. The Judge sustains the Exceptions & directs the Court below to proceed.

Signed.   Th° P. Carnes

I do certify that the above is a true Extract from the Minutes.

Ed^w Adams for Ge° Taylor, Clk, S. C. J. C.

Wm Parker   }
     vs   }
John McCune }

Jury N° 2

We, the Jury, find for the plaintiff forty four Dollars twelve & half Cents, with Cost.

                                     Wm Strong, F. M.

Uriah Humphries }
     vs   }
Ge° McFalls   }

Jury N° 2

We find for the plaintiff the Sum of Ninety Nine Dollars & Eighty Cents, with Interest & Costs.

Wm Strong, F. M.

Court Adjourned till tomorrow Ten o'clock.

Thursday 29 Jany 1801, 10 o'clock A. M.

The Court Met, on the bench   B. Benge
                                             A. Ramey &
                                             J. L. Pittman, Esquires.

The following Jury sworn generally

1. Abednego Moore
2. Alex^r Mchard
3. Wm Robertson
4. Ed Edwards
5. ~~Robt McGowin~~ Matt Hawkins
6. Thos Hightower
7. Thos Bankston
8. Benjn Easley
9. Burket Dean
10. Wm Ramey
11. Wm Foster
12. Thos Hill

William Scott }
    vs   }
John Alexander }
& Robt Barber }

Nonsuit.

Micajah W^{m}son }
    vs   } Att^t
William Few   }

Dismissed by the plaintiff.

Ignatius Few came into Court & enter'd him Special Bail in the Above case, to witt, he the party defendant Shall pay the eventual condemnation money, if Any, he will do it for him, or Render his Body to the common Jail of this County, in discharge of himself, when Shall be charged in Execution.

I. Few

Test. W. Pentecost, Clk

Robt McGowin }
    vs   }
Harmon Runnels }

Jury N° 1 Sworn Generally

We, the Jury, find for the Plaintiff the sum of Two hundred & fifty Six Dollars, with Interest & Cost of Suit.

Signed.   B. Easly, f. M.

———

Eli Evanson }
    vs   } Judgment
John Depriest }

William Daniel came to the Office & enter'd himself Security, in Double the sum Mentioned in this Judgment, for Stay of Execution Sixty Days, According to Law.

Wm Daniel

Test. W. Pentecost

Order'd, that William Potts, Esqr, Collector of Taxes, pay over to Charles Daugharty, Esqr the Sum of Seventy two Dollars & thirty Cents, when he shall have Collected the Money, for the purpose of Erecting Bridges.

———

I, Thomas Reynolds, do Solemnly Swear that I will faithfully Execute all Writs & Warrants, precepts & processes Directed to me as Deputy Sheriff of the County of Jackson, & True Returns Make, and in all things Will & Truly, without Malice or partiality, perform the Duties office of Deputy Sheriff, During my Continuance in office, & take only my Lawfull fees, so help me God.

Thos Reynolds

Test.

B. Harris, J. I. C^t
Absolom Ramey, J. I. C^t
Micajah Benge, J. I. C^t

N° 2. On the petition of Sundry Inhabitants of this County, praying that the Commissioners formerly appointed to lay out a Road from Fitz Patrick's ferry on the Oconee to the Beach Creek Settlement, be directed to Review that part of said Road that is at or near Barber's Creek & find, if convenient, a more fitting ford on the said Creek, & that Commissioners be appointed on the Mulberry fork to extend the same to the Upper Settlements

---

of said County. Ordered, that the Petition be Granted & that William Pentecost, George Reid, & Hugh Montgomery, Esquires be added to that Number.

3. Ordered, that Willoughby Hammock & William Duke be appointed Justices of the Peace for the Ninth District of the Second Battalion of the Jackson County Militia.

Ordered, That John Billups & Talbot Arthur be appointed Overseers of the Road leading from the Cedar Shoals on the North Oconee to the Cherokee Corner, as hath been hitherto laid Out, & that all persons within four Miles of said Road be liable to work thereon, when Required by the said Overseers.

5. Ordered, that a Road be laid out from Pope's ford on the Oconee River, the nearest & best way, to where it will entersect with a Road already laid out, leading through Oglethorpe County, & crossing Cloud's Creek at Gorden's Iron Works, & that James Mayes, Joseph East, & Abnor James be Commissioners

---

to lay out & Report thereon to the next Court.

7. Ordered, that Two Children named Marget Leor & Salley Leor be bound to Robert Boyd 'till they shall become of Lawful Age, he complying with the

requisits of the Law & enter into Bond, with Security, before the Clerk of this Court.

8. Ordered, that a Road be laid out from Clarksborough the nearest & best way to Melone's Mill, & from thence on a direction for Finizy's as fare as the County line, & that [blot], John Nall, & Jerry Matthews be the Surveyors to lay out the same, from Clarksborough to the River, & John Cunningham, David Harris, & William Strong, Esquires lay out the S^d Road from thence to the County line.

9. Ordered, that Eli Whaley be appointed Overseer of the Road leading from Beach Creek to Esquire Hubbard's, in the place of Luke Durbin, resigned.

10. Ordered, that William Deal be appointed Overseer of the Road leading from Clarksborough to the dividing ridge on the temporary line between the North fork of the Oconee & Candler's Creek.

11th Ordered, that the undertakers bound to erect the & compleat the Court House do proceed to have the same fully compleated on or before the next Superior Court, to be held in & for this County, Otherwise, the Court will proceed agreeable to Law, & that Rodrick Easley, Esquire be served with this Order in ten days.

12. Ordered, that the sum of Ten dollars each be allowed Edmond Edwards, Thomas Hill, & William Robertson, for their faithful services as Commissioners in Keeping Open the Oconee River agreeable to Law, & be it further Ordered, that Johnson Strong, Esqr be added as a Commissioner for the same purpose.

13. Ordered, that a Road be reviewed & laid out, from the Store of Vann & Davis, near where the State line Crosses Allen's fork, the nearest & best way, to Jackson Court House, under the same regulations as Other Roads Are, & that Thomas Kirkpatrick, John Hill,

---

John Townsend, John Depriest, & Theophilus Hickmon be the Commissioners to lay out the same & report thereon.

14. Ordered, that John Barron be appointed Overseer of the Road leading from the Court House to Beach Creek, in the place of Edwd Williams.

15. Ordered, that the Clerk of this Court do call on the Collector for the County Tax for the Year One thousand Seven hundred & Ninety Nine & that he report to the Adjourned Court.

16. Ordered, that Gabriel Hubbard & Richard Easley be appointed Justices of the peace in [blank] district.

17. Ordered, that the sum of fifteen Dollars & 24 Cents be put into the Hands of Thos Hill for the use of Mrs Stedman.

18. Ordered, that William Daniel, Esquire, Collector of Taxes for the Year 1799, put into the Hands of Thomas Hill, Overseer of the Poor, Thirty Dollars, for the Use of the Mackee's.

---

19. Ordered, that William Daniel be appointed a Justice of the Peace, in the place of John Mayes, Esquire, who has removed.

William Gough }
    vs   } Judgment
James Stringer }

James Stringer came by his friend, Gabriel Hubbard, & paid the Cost that had arisen, & prayed an appeal, when Gabriel Hubbard acknowledged himself Security, that is, the Defendant shall pay the eventual condemnation Money, if any, he will do it for him, or Render the defendant to the Common Jail, in discharge of himself, when the defendant is charged in execution.

                                                Gab^l Hubert

Test. W. Pentecost, Clk

---

20. Ordered, that the Collector of Taxes for the County of Jackson for the Year 1801, be Authorized & directed to Levy & Collect a Tax equal to One Sixth of General Tax for the use of said County. Also, one fourteenth part for the use of the Poor of Said County. And, also one tenth for the purpose of erecting a Bridge on the poast Road, across the Oconee River, at the place known by the name of King's Bridge, & that Joseph Humphress, John Hampton, & John King, Esquires

be appointed Commissioners to All the building & Keeping in repair the Said Bridge for the Term of five Years.

21. Whereas, the Laws of this State make it the duty of the Several Inferior Courts to define & Apportion the Hands subject to work on the several Roads in the respective Counties, & whereas the Court has not Sufficient information to enable them to comply with that part of the Law. Therefore, be it Ordered, that the several Overseers heretofore appointed be Authorized & directed to call on all persons who may be residenters within

———

four Miles of any Road, that do not work on any other Publick Road, shall be liable & obliged to work on all such Roads, & Subject to all the fines & penalties annexed by the said Laws, & that the said Overseers are hereby required & directed to compell the Attendance of all such persons, & to Act in all other respects agreeable to Law, & that the Clerk is hereby directed to furnish the Overseers with a True Copy of this Order.

22. Whereas, the Inferior Court, at June Term 1800, did pass an Order & Directed a Tax to be Levyed Equal to One Sixth of the General tax, for the purpose of erecting two Publick Bridges, & the Court at the present term, having taken into consideration that the Said Sum would be inadequate to the said undertaking, & for the Court to discharge the several demands made Against the County, which they Ought in good faith to discharge; Ordered, therefore, that the Tax Leveyed as aforsaid be applyed for other purposes as the Court may direct.

———

[at least two pages apparently missing]

———

Deal, & William Willson do lay out the same, & that John Moore be appointed overseer to open the said Road.

Ordered, that James Barr, David Castleberry, & David Walker be appointed Commissioners to lay out a Road from the flat Shoals to the North Oconee River, to William Gilbert's near the County line, & Report thereon.

Ordered, that William Reed & J[blot] James Stean be appointed Justices of the Peace, for the County of Jackson, in Capt Hendricks' Company, in the room of James Hendricks, appointed Judge of the Inferior Court, & William Laurence, resigned.

Ordered, that Parks Chandler be appointed a Justice of the peace in Capt Harris's Company, in the room of John M. Carter, Resigned.

Joseph Smith & }
Brooks Mottersherd }
    vs } Judg^t $44.21¼
John Woods }

John Woods Came to the Office, paid the Cost which had arisen, & prayed an Appeal, when Archerbald Nelson entered himself Security, that is to say, he the said John Woods shall pay the eventual Condemnation money, if any, he will do it for him, or deliver his Body to the Common Jail of this County, when he the Defendant Shall be charged in Execution.

                        Arch^d Nelson

W. Pentecost, Clk

~~Ordered, that Isaac Hill be appointed Overseer of the Road Leading from Clarksborough to Van's Store, on that part that Johnson Clark was Overseer on, & the same Hands to work under him that formerly Worked under said Clark.~~ The above was entered before.

Samuel Gardnor, Ass^{ee} }
of Ambrose Camron }
    vs }
John Armour & }
Wm Cain }

John Armour Came to the Office, paid the Cost that had Accrued, & prayed an Appeal, when Thomas Colbert entered himself Security, that is to say, he the said John shall pay the eventual Condemnation Money, if any, he will do it for him, or deliver his Body to the Common Jail of this County, when he the Defendant Shall be Charged in Execution.

Thomas Colbert

W. Pentecost, Clk

Court Adjourned till the Second Monday in March

W. Pentecost, Clk

———

[at least one page missing]

~~ordered that~~ Whereas, Nathaniel Jones Did on the fifth day of October 1798, With Several Securities, enter into an Obligation for the Completion of a Court house & Jail, as also to Make Good & Sufficient Titles to Ten acres of Land for the use of an Academy, as well as to support the Titles for the Public Buildings, and whereas, the said Jones has allege then failed in his said Contract, & the Court having no assurances for the Security of the Compliance of the said obligation, it is ordered that, unless the said Contract is Complied with During the Siting of this Court agreeable to their former order, the Court Will proceed to Erect Buildings at Some other places, as they Have not as yet Disposed of any more of the Publick funds of this County than they will Replace from their own private property.

Test. W. Pentecost, Clk

———

~~John Branham~~

June Term 1801

Benjamin Branham }
      vs   }
Daniel W. Easley }

Setled at Defendant's Cost & the Cost paid.

Paid the same to Peterson Thweatt as p^r Order filed in the Original Declaration, to Wit, One hundred & Eighty four Dollars& nine Cents.

W. Pentecost, Clk

Am^t of Note & }
Interest } $184.09

[smudge] 1798

The Inferior Court [smudge]
for 2 quire paper $1.00
  1 d^o 47

~~McKe~~	191.59½	
~~vs~~	192.81	
~~T. Kenerly~~	1.22½	
	50	
	1.72½	

(Sup^r Court)

Rec^d of A. Ramey for [light] $8.56
of J. Humphress for D^o 2.56
Rec^d of ~~William Daniel~~ Alex^r Harper 12.00

Paid to the Sheriff (T. Runels) 16.81

Rec^d of Esqr McColphin 10.75 for estrays
  of Hugh Montgomery 14.48¼
  of Johnson Strong 10.70
  [scratched out]
  of John Diamond 3.75
  [faint] 8.56
  of Shepperd for Tavern 8.56
  of Jones L. Clark
  Cont Ben Easley [blot] 47.85¼
  [blot] Blackburn

[faint] Rec^d of Esqr Easley }
[faint]   }   5.00

Lotts sold by the County

N° 5 To Benjn Easley for $113.00
       6 To David Witt for   60.00
       1&7 To John Diamond
           for 38 & 60 Dollars   98.00
      11 To Bledsoe for   95.00
      35 To William Stubblefield for   41.00
          Total Am^t $407.00

~~Rec^d 28th September 1801~~
~~of Esquire Thurmond five Dollars~~
~~Six & one fourth Cents~~   4.06¼
~~[torn]f Mr Loyd for License~~   0.56¼
[torn]^d Hunton 3 Doll^s Total   12.62¼
[torn]^d Stewert 3.37½
[torn]^d Richd Wood for Richd Easley 2.50
[torn]^d Potts for Aaron Wood 1.25
[torn]^d Shackleford 4.00

28th September 1801

Of Esquire Thurmond for Estrays Sold by him   4.06
Of Mr Loyd for Tavern Licence   8.56
Of Capt Hunton for Tavern Licence   8.56
Of John Nalls   8.56
Total up to Novr 7th 1801   29.74
Due me up to the Nov^r [faint] $37.62

Robert McGowin }
     vs   } Judgment
Harmon Runels }

Runnels

In the Above case, Preston Runnels came into the Office & acknowledged himself Security, in Double the Sum mentioned in this Judgment, for Stay of Execution Sixty days, Agreeable to the Act of Assembly in Such cases made & provided, Viz^t. he, the Defendant, Shall pay the Am^t of said Judgment, he will do it for him.

Signed.   Preston Runnels

Test. W. Pentecost, Clk

                                B. Harris, J. I. C^t
                                J. Pittman, J. I. C^t
                                Absalom Ramey, J. P.

March the 24th 1801

The following Jury Drawn in the Presence of their Honors Bucknor Harris & James Pittman, Esquires, to wit.

1. Lewis Hinor
2. Jessee Morgan
3. Benjn Watkins
4. John McVay
5. Benjn Vermillion
6. John Pakston
7. Thomas Crane
8. John Sawyer
9. Morrill Thomas
10. John Hill
11. Gilbert Mash
12. Wm Carter
13. Randolph Traylor
14. Saml Hopkins
15. John Hinton
16. Asa Hamilton
17. Owen L. Boing
18. Uriah Humphress
19. Isaac Lee
22. James King
23. James Cuningham
24. Wm Marble
25. Prior Thornton
26. Wm Stone
27. John Moss
28. Wm Jackson
29. Richd Anderson
30. Garratt Park
31. Jno Tidwell
32. David Luckie
33. William Davis
34. John Kimbrill
35. Sherrod Strong
36. Sherwood Horton
37. James Beasley
38. Bosnon O'Dear
39. Matt Anderson
40. John Webb

20. Thº Phelps
21. Edward Edwards

41. Chaˢ Jent
42. Josh Hightower
43. Geº Ewings
44. John Muckleham
45. John Adams
46. Arthur Taylor
47. Wᵐ Akin
48. Thº Hinton

[the following page appears to be out of order]

Jnº Woods Mark is crop & Slit in each ear July 27, 1797

Traylor returns 3.54

John Cuningham returns 4 Dollars
for Estrays sold by him   4.00
Hugh Montgomery   3 Dollars
Robᵗ McColpen, Esqʳ   17.87½
Esqʳ Rogers   9.22
Esqʳ Strong   ~~85.79~~
                         ~~89~~ 7.40
                                78.29

200.54
 80.78
290.37
246.68
 43.64   Estrays $39.34

Licence to Ector   8.56
       to Gardner   8.56
                         $56.46

Index

   Isaac, 59
   Nathan, 59
   Thos., 67
   Tom, 49
Adams
   Edw., 80
   Edwd., 49
   James, 49
   John, 42, 43, 92
   Thomas, 48
Adare
   Bozmon, 35, 49
Akin
   William, 37, 41, 43
   Wm., 92
Akins
   William, 36
Alexander, 43
   Edmund, 9, 12, 15
   Elias, 67
   John, 81
Allen, 46, 84
   James, 49
Anderson
   Ben, 71
   Jordan, 24, 28
   Jorden, 28
   Jordon, 6
   Matt, 91
   Richard, 29
   Richd., 22, 29, 91
Armour
   John, 57, 87
Armstrong
   James, 25, 32, 80

   Jas., 6
   Jas., Sr., 71
   Jesse, 32
   Jno., 38
   John, 38
   Ludwell, 30, 32, 49
Arther
   Talbert, 79
Arthur
   Talbert, 71, 72, 76
   Talbot, 37, 38, 62, 73, 83
Awtrey
   Absalem, 48
Bailey
   John, 65
Bankston
   Abner, 34, 48, 74
   Daniel, 62
   Jacob, 68, 72
   Jas., 66
   Thos., 81
   William, 47
Barber, 83
   Robt., 81
Barnet, 33, 48
   John, 47, 48, 66
   Miles, 47
   Saml., 71
Barnett, 60
   Jno., 9, 16
   John, 5, 7, 8, 16, 32
   Mial, 6
Barr
   James, 86
Barron
   John, 84

Thomas, 33
Beal, 58
Bearden, 59, 60
  Arthur, 65
Beasley
  James, 91
Bell, 19
  Walter, 6, 7, 42, 74, 79
Benge
  B., 81
  Micaijah, 40, 72
  Micajah, 19, 37, 45, 72, 73, 83
  Micijah, 35
Benton
  Thos., 64
Best
  Saml., 6
Biggerstaff
  John, 65
Billups
  John, 83
Black
  Jno., 71
  John, 44, 70
  William, 65
Blackburn, 89
  Augustin, Jr., 65
  Augustine, 27
  Elizabeth, 27
  Nancy, 27
  Sarah, 27
  William, 27
  Wm., 65
Blackburne
  Augustine, 11, 20
Blake
  William, 34
  Wm., 60
Bledsoe, 90
Bogs

James, 59
Boing
  Owen L., 91
Boren
  Isaac, 34
Bowman
  Ezekiel, 59
Boyd
  Robert, 83
  Wm., Sr., 60
Bradshaw
  Jno., 6, 7, 71, 74
  John, 73
  Thos., 30, 65
Brand
  William, 32
Branham
  Benjamin, 88
  John, 66, 88
Branum
  John, 70
Braswell
  Allen, 71
Brazel
  Allen, 42
Brewer
  Orsbourn, 56
Briant
  William, 65
Briars
  Laurence, 8, 14
Bridgewater
  Samuel, 5
Britain
  James, 62
Brooks
  Middleton, 60
Brown, 39
  Bedford, 38, 39
  David, 51

Hewety, 60
Thomas, 47
William, 7, 51
Wm., 5
Browning
  Benjamin, 59
  Joshua, 16
Buckels
  Peter, 74
Burch
  Miles, 30
Burford
  Will, 69
Burk
  Robert, 65
  Thos., 65, 66
Burks
  Thos., 16
Butler
  George, 71
Cade
  Wm., 37
Cagle
  Roger, 47
Caid
  William, 42
Cain
  Jessee, 65
  Wm., 57, 87
Calahan
  Jas., 67
Calehan
  Edward, 50
Calhoon, 30
  Hugh, 30
Callehans
  Edwd., 50
Cameron
  Ambrose, 27
Cammeron

Ambrose, 27
Camp, 60
  Stephen, 42
  William, 34
Campbell, 43
  Robert, 43, 62, 63, 75
  Robt., 62
Camron
  Ambros, 47
  Ambrose, 87
  John, 51
  Thos., 51
Candler, 59, 69, 84
Carlile
  Edmond, 43
Carmichael
  John, 60
Carnes
  T. P., 23
  Tho. P., 80
  Thos. P., 5, 20
Carson
  Joseph, 74
Carter, 40, 55
  Jacob, 20, 22, 24, 29, 30
  Jno. Martin, 72
  John M., 43, 55, 87
  John Martin, 69
  Thos., 21, 24
  William, 50
  Wm., 5, 61, 91
Casey
  Jesse, 41
  John, 59
  Wm., 60
Castleberry
  David, 86
Cathey
  George, 47
Cawthorn

95

Wm., 6
Chandler, 50
  Parks, 65, 66, 87
Chapman
  John, 63
Clark, 42, 54
  Johnson, 5, 20, 34, 46, 87
  Johnston, 54
  Jones L., 89
  Jordain, 37, 57
Clarkson
  Joseph, 79
Clerk, 41
Cloud, 83
Coasey
  Samuel, 60
Cockran
  James, 68
Colb
  Peter, 72
Colbert
  Thomas, 87, 88
  Thos., 37
Collins
  Zachariah, 54
  Zackh., 52
Com___
  Andrew, 49
Compton
  Bonner, 66
Connel
  Walter, 49
Cook
  Jonathan, 59
Coone
  Henry, 35
Cosby, 58, 76, 77
Cowan
  George, 53
Cowen, 49

Alexander, 60
  Geo., 53
  George, 52
Crane
  Tho., 35
  Thomas, 91
  Thos., 37
Crawford, 60
Crawley
  Saml., 47
Criswell, 59
  David, 51
Crowley
  Saml., 24, 25, 28
Cuningham
  Geo., 10, 15
  James, 91
  Jas., 52
  Jno., 6, 7, 9, 16, 25
  John, 8, 92
Cunningham
  G. P., 32
  George, 21, 24
  J. N., 32
  James, 53
  John, 84
Cup
  Michael, 16
Curington
  William, 79
Curnton
  William, 72
  Wm., 71, 74
Curry, 46
Daniel
  William, 82, 85, 89
  William, Jr., 62
  Wm., 82
Daugharty
  Charles, 82

Davis, 46, 84
  Joseph, 46
  William, 91
Deal, 69, 86
  William, 49, 66, 84
  Wm., 66
Dean
  Burket, 79, 81
Deane
  Nathaniel, 47
Depriest
  Jno., 74
  John, 52, 71, 72, 77, 82, 84
Diamond
  Jno., 67
  John, 46, 52, 68, 78, 89, 90
  Robert, 65
Dickson
  Wm., 60
Dimond
  John, 71, 76
Dixon
  J. Henry, 45
Doss
  Mark, 60
Dougherty
  Chs., 32, 62
Dowdle
  B. J., 75
Downs
  Silas, 48
Dubose
  James, 56
Duke
  Thos., 23
  William, 14, 83
  Wm., 6, 7, 15
Dukes
  Jno., 10, 15
Durbin

  Luke, 73, 84
Easley, 12, 33, 90
  B., 13, 14, 17, 18, 19, 20, 24, 26,
    28, 29, 31, 33, 63, 64
  Ben, 16, 89
  Benjn., 81, 90
  D. W., 6, 7, 8, 9, 10, 12, 13, 14,
    16, 17, 18, 19, 27
  Daniel, 40
  Daniel W., 55, 70, 88
  Danl. W., 5
  Jeffery, 74
  R., 79
  Richard, 39, 44, 45, 62, 70, 79, 85
  Richd., 34, 36, 39, 44, 68, 72, 76,
    77, 90
  Rk., 26
  Roderick, 33
  Rodk., 5, 14, 17, 19, 24, 26, 29,
    32, 34, 40, 55, 69
  Rodrick, 55, 84
  W., 28, 55
Easly
  B., 82
East, 51
  Jas., 5
  Joseph, 10, 15, 19, 83
Eastice
  John, 66
Eavenson
  Eli, 77
Ector, 92
Edmonds
  Edmd., 36
Edwards, 60
  Ed, 81
  Edmond, 40, 42, 84
  Edmund, 80
  Edward, 92
  Edwd., 37

Elam
  James, 76
Ellisson
  Robt., 76
Elsberry
  Jeremh., 65
Ely
  Wm., 25
Emet
  Jas., 25
Espy
  John, 19, 63
Evanson
  Eli, 82
Ewing
  Geo., 36, 42
  George, 37
  Jas., 41
Ewings
  Geo., 92
  George, 36
Faulkenberry
  Jacob, 49
  John, 49
Few
  I., 82
  Ignatius, 82
  William, 81
  Wm., 68
Fielder
  Jno., 71
  John, 16
  William, 31
Finch
  ___, 59
  Rasberry, 60
Findley
  James, 78
Finizy, 84
Finley
  Mathew, 11, 21
Fitzpatrick, 83
Flemming
  Peter, 31
Floyd, 48
Forsythe
  Jacob, 67
Fortenbury
  Robt., 25
Fortinberry
  Rot., 25
Foster
  Arthur, 54
  George, 69
  William, 51, 54, 69
  Wm., 81
Freeman
  Ben, 66
  Benjn., 65
Fulgen
  Ephraim, 65
Gann
  Nathan, 38
Gardner, 60, 92
  Levi, 56
  Martin, 21, 24
  Saml., 32, 33, 40, 57, 75, 78
  Samuel, 61
Gardnor
  Samuel, 87
Gathright
  M., 21, 22, 25
  Miles, 6, 17, 20, 24, 33
Geddian
  James, 71
Gent
  Charles, 30, 32, 36
  Chas., 37, 40
Gentry
  Cain, 6, 53

Elijah, 16
Elisha, 30, 32
Wm., 6, 65, 67
Gentt
　Charles, 42
George
　Jno., 26
　John, 26
　Thomas, 45
Gilaspy
　Daniel, 47
Gilbert
　William, 86
Glen
　James, 76
Glenn
　James, 71
Gorden, 35, 83
　Frances, 29
　Francis, 12, 13, 22, 23, 29
Gordon
　Francis, 19
Gough
　William, 85
　Wm., 78
Gray, 52, 58
　William, 49
Green, 56
　Jas., 47
　Jno., 74
　John, 53, 58
　Wm., 75
Greene
　James, 72
　John, 52, 57
Greenwood, 60
Griffin, 73
　Jno., 30
　John, 73, 74, 78
Grisham

Edmund, 60
Jas., 20
Jno., 11
John, 8, 28
Hagler
　Peter, 62
Hagood
　Benjamin, 48
Halcoor
　Absalom, 6
Hall, 58
Hamilton
　Asa, 6, 91
　John, Jr., 60
　William, 78
Hammock
　Willoughby, 83
Hampton
　Jno., 75
　John, 85
Hancock
　Martin, 49
Haney
　Geo., 16
　George, 36
Hannah
　Wm., 65
Hansel
　Jno, 71
　John, 64
Harden
　Swan, 65
Hardin
　Susan, 27
Hargrave
　Eldridge, 46
Hargrove
　Eldridge, 46, 57
Harper, 78
　Alexander, 28

Alexr., 89
Elexr., 71
Geo., 63
James, 7, 43
Jas., 6, 7
Harris, 55, 87
  B., 61, 64, 65, 68, 73, 75, 79, 83, 91
  Buckner, 45, 55
  Bucknor, 64, 65, 67, 72, 91
  Bucr., 66
  David, 84
Harriss, 40
  B., 35, 45, 54
  Buckner, 35
  Bucknor, 37, 40, 51, 72
  Thomas, 41
  Thos., 41
Hart
  John, 16, 27, 51
Hathorn
  James, 49
Hawkins
  Matt, 81
Hays
  George, 21, 24
Head
  Daniel, 80
  Danl., 35, 39
  William, Jr., 15
Heart
  John, 5
Henderson
  James, 16
  John, 46
  Jones, 41, 42
  Saml., 34, 67
Hendon
  Elijah, 15, 16, 74
  Isham, 27

Hendrick, 69
Hendricks, 51, 87
  Elizabeth, 58
  James, 69, 87
  Jas., 65
  Jno., 54
Henry
  George, 33
Herd
  Stephen, 30
Hickey
  Elizabeth, 17
Hickmon
  Theophilus, 84
Higgins, 50
  John, 50
Hightower
  Josh, 92
  Joshua, 8, 11, 20, 28, 36, 37, 41, 42
  Thos., 8, 11, 20, 21, 28, 81
Hill
  Isaac, 6, 7, 47, 54, 75, 87
  James, 47, 76
  John, 84, 91
  Nathaniel, 52, 53, 77
  Thomas, 48, 70, 84, 85
  Thos., 38, 81, 85
Hills
  Isaac, 33
  Thomas, 33
Hinor
  Lewis, 91
Hinton
  John, 35, 37, 91
  Tho., 92
  Thos., 36, 37
Hobson, 60
Hodge, 56, 73
  Elliott, 54

William, 34
Hog
  Thomas, 34
Holland
  John, 50
  Sewil, 65
  Thomas, 60
Holliday
  Jeremiah, 66
Holms
  James, 50
Hoover
  Jacob, 50
Hopkins, 69
  Jno., 15
  John, 10
  Richard, 16
  Saml., 91
  William, 16, 43
  Wm., 21
Hopper
  Thos., 65
Horton
  John, 66
  Proser, 57
  Prosor, 37, 40, 42
  Prosser, 36
  Sherwood, 35, 37, 40, 42, 91
House, 60
Housler
  Jacob, 6
Houver
  Jacob, 20, 24
Hubbard, 84
  Gabl., 48, 72
  Gabriel, 68, 85
Hubert
  Gabl., 85
Hudson, 47
Huie

James, 68
Humphres
  Uriah, 79
Humphress
  J., 89
  Joseph, 70, 85
  Uriah, 35, 36, 37, 91
Humphrey
  Joseph, 50
Humphreys
  Joseph, 18, 53
Humphries
  J. L., 5
  Jos., 10, 19, 23
  Joseph, 5, 6, 9, 10, 14, 17, 20, 23, 24, 27
  Uriah, 33, 74, 80
Hunton, 90
Huston
  John, 47
Hutchinson
  William, 10
  Wm., 10, 11, 15
Hych
  Thomas, 79
  Thos., 30, 32
Irving
  James, 49
Ivy
  Isaac, 59
J___, 87
Jackson
  Stephen, 57
  Wm., 91
James
  Abner, 20
  Abnor, 35, 71, 83
Jenkins
  Jesse, 47
Jent

Chas., 92
Jentry
  Cain, 17, 48
  Elige, 47
Jeter
  Andrew, 56
Jether
  Andrew, 21
Jewel
  J., 77
Johnson, 49
  John H., 49
  Tho., 75
  Thomas, 42
  Thos., 65
Johnston
  Robt., 52
Jones, 11, 88
  Basil, 11
  Bazil, 20
  Nathaniel, 88
  Rus, 40
  Russel, 56
  Thos., 53, 54
  Wm., 20, 24
Kagle
  Roger, 45
Keeth
  George, 46
Kellet
  Joseph, 52
  William, 59
Kellett
  Joseph, 53
  William, 59
Kenerly
  Jno., 12
  John, 7
  T., 89
  Thos., 6

Kennedy
  George, 79
Kennerley
  John, 5, 31, 37
  Thos., 31
Kennerly
  George, 6
  John, 31, 42
  Thos., 14
Killett
  Joseph, 53
Killough, 47
  Allen, 48, 65
  Isaac, 47
  Jas., 47
  Saml., 73
  Tho., 47
  Thomas, 34
Killpatrick, 26
Kilough, 19
  Allen, 66
  Davd., 21
  David, 6, 10, 12, 15
  Saml., 6, 7, 21, 25
  Samuel, 34
Kilpatrick
  Thos., 10
Kimbrill
  John, 91
King, 85
  James, 91
  Jno., 26
  John, 27, 85
  Joseph, 27
Kirkland
  Wm., 71
Kirkpatrick, 16, 19, 48
  Jas., 42
  Tho., 54
  Thomas, 51, 52, 80, 84

Thos., 15, 19, 26, 46, 67
Kneal
  William, 49
Knight
  Matt, 57
  Matthew, 45
Knox
  Benja., 15
  Benjamin, 13
  James, 75
  Saml., 6, 10, 11, 13, 16, 25
  Samuel, 5, 8, 11, 13
Kurrey, 26
Lackey
  James, 48
Lancaster, 46
  Joseph, 49
Landrith
  Moses, 62
Lane
  Jonathan, 10, 15, 21, 24, 37
  Joseph, 79
Lankford
  Peter, 60
  Robert, 60
Laren
  Olliver, 49
Laron
  Oliver, 30, 32
Laughridge
  James, 21
  Jas., 32
Laurence
  William, 51, 87
  Wm., 69
Laymaster
  Joseph, 57, 58
Ledbetter
  Buck, 25
  Henry, 6

Lee
  Isaac, 91
Lemmond
  Joseph, 42
Leor
  Marget, 83
  Salley, 83
Light
  Obadiah, 58, 60
  Obediah, 65
Lindsay
  Abraham, 58
  Ephraim, 53
  Jacob, 54
  Joseph, 58
Lindsey
  Jac., 43
  Jacob, 34, 41, 42, 43, 44
  James, 36
Linsley
  John, 34
Little
  Saml., 37
Long
  Saml., 47
Loving
  Gabriel, 49
Lowry, 60
Loyd, 90
  William, 48
  Wm., 68
Luckey
  David, 26
Luckie
  David, 6, 35, 37, 91
Lucky
  John, 73
Lukie
  Isaac, 47
Lynch

Robert, 56
M__
  Wm., 60
M'Vay
  John, 35
Mackee, 85
Maharge
  Elex, 71
Marble
  Wm., 91
Martin, 40
  Catchwns, 60
  John, 60
Mash
  Gilbert, 91
Mathews, 17
  Danl., 6, 25
Matthews
  Danl., 65
  George, 50, 69
  Jerry, 84
  William, 34, 50
Mayes
  James, 83
  John, 85
Mayo
  John, 61
McAlpin, 62
  Robert, 30
McCarter
  Jeremiah J., 27
  Nancy, 27
McCartney
  Jno., 21, 24
McClendon
  Mark, 69
McClusky
  James, 34
McColpen
  Robt., 92

McColphin, 50, 89
McConnell
  J., 45
  John, 42
McConnis
  John, Jr., 60
McCord
  David, 50
  Robert, 51, 63
  Robt., 51
McCorkle
  William, 60
McCoy
  Henry, 79
McCright, 47
  Quinton, 51
McCune
  John, 80
McCutchin
  Jos., 23
  Joseph, 19, 26, 32, 57
McCutchins
  Jos., 70
McDermont, 60
McDonald
  Alexander, 57
McElhannon, 60
  John, 60
McFall, 46
  Geo., 77
McFalls, 58
  Geo., 6, 66, 70, 80
  George, 12, 23
  Jno., 19
  John, 47
McFeld, 47
McGowin
  Robert, 90
  Robt., 7, 67, 68, 70, 74, 81, 82
McGown

Robert, 80
Mchard
  Alexander, 76
  Alexr., 81
McHard
  Alexandr., 76
McHead
  Alexander, 79
McIver
  John, 63
McKe, 89
McKee
  Wm., 14
McMullin, 32
  James J., 56
McNab
  Andrew, 31
McNabb
  Andrew, 7, 12
McNeely
  David, 76
McVay
  Hugh, 36, 37
  John, 37, 41, 42, 91
McWright
  Jas., 51
Medlock
  Nathl., 6
Mehargue
  Alexander, 72
Melon, 50
Melone, 84
  Jno., 77
  John, 33, 47
  William, 70
Miars
  Heny., 49
Michael, 11
  Jno., 11
Midlebroks

Isaac, 32
Midlebrook
  Isaac, 6
Miller
  ___, 59
  Andrew, 49, 71, 73, 76
  Charles, 60
  Ebenezer, 60
  James, 13, 50
  Jno., 6, 7, 13, 19, 20
  Peter, 51
  Wm., 60
Milton
  William, 57
Mobley
  Eleazer, 63
  Jethro, 63
Mobly
  Jethro, 78
Montgomery
  H., 52, 54, 55
  Hugh, 52, 54, 63, 83, 89, 92
  James, 43, 63
  Robert, 46, 54, 60
Montgomry
  James, 34
Mooney
  Obriant, 5
Moore
  Abed, 71
  Abednego, 72, 74, 79, 81
  John, 52, 53, 54, 86
  Mathew, 6
  Michael, 52, 53
Moote
  Silas, 51
Morgan
  Jessee, 91
  Stephen, 65
Morison, 19

Alexr., 25
Morris
  Chesley, 6, 7
Morrison
  Alexander, 51
  Alexr., 19, 21
Morriss
  Ruth, 76
  Tho., 76
Morrisson, 16
Mortin
  Josiah, 66
Morton
  J., 67
  Jacob, 48
  Joseph, 65
  Josiah, 27, 66
Moss
  Jno., 14
  John, 8, 35, 91
  Littleton, 50
Mothershed
  Brook, 53
Mottersheard
  Brooks, 42
Mottersherd
  Brooks, 37, 79, 87
Muckelhannon
  John, 60
Muckleham
  John, 92
Nall
  John, 12, 26, 76, 79, 84
  M., 74, 75, 76, 77, 79
  Martin, 19, 31, 74, 78, 79
  William, 19
Nalls, 90
  John, 12
  Martin, 31, 47
Nash

James, 46
Nation
  Joseph, 42
Nelson
  Archd., 87
  Archerbald, 87
  Jno., 6
  Samuel, 54
  Thos., 6
Niblack
  Saml., 71
Nichols
  Wm., 10
Nobles
  Jonathan, 75
  Robert, 42
  Stephen, 48
O'Dear
  Bosnon, 91
  Bozman, 37
Oliver
  James B., 21
Ollive
  Anthony, 75
Oneal
  Ruth, 76
Ostean
  Jesse, 49
Pace
  Isaac, 49
  James, 49
  William, 49
Pakston
  John, 91
Park
  Ezekl. B., 71
  Garratt, 91
  Jas., 65
  John, 30
  Wm., 74

Parker, 59
  Wm., 80
Parks, 43
  Garret, 35, 76
  James, 30, 35
  Jas., 31, 67
  Jno., 6, 7, 31
  John, 30, 79
  Thomas, 46
  William, 34, 43, 44
Parr
  Ben, 16
  Benjamin, 29
Party
  Jno., 6
Patrick
  Luke, 25
  Paul, 19, 61
Pattern
  Arthur, 10, 13, 14, 15, 27
  Saml., 13, 21
  Samuel, 32
  Solomon, 14
  Wm., 21, 24
Patton
  Arthur, 37, 38
Peck
  Judith, 54
Penington
  Isaac, 74
  John, 40
Penn
  Edmund, 55
Pentecost
  W., 35, 39, 41, 44, 45, 58, 66, 68, 75, 82, 85, 87, 88, 89, 91
  William, 83
  Wm., 62
Peron
  Lewis, 66
Pettyjohn
  Jacob, 46
Phair
  Jonathan, 49, 50
Pharr
  Edward, 61
  Jonathan, 61
Phelps
  Tho., 92
Philip, 48
Philips
  George, 77
Phillips
  Edmund, 13
  Edward, 32
Phinizy, 47
Pinkston
  Danl., 49
Pitman
  James, 5, 9, 45, 71
  Jas., 5, 68
Pittman
  J., 26, 28, 32, 75, 91
  J. L., 81
  James, 10, 14, 17, 18, 19, 23, 26, 29, 32, 40, 45, 51, 73, 91
  Jas., 10, 19, 24, 35, 37, 54, 61, 64, 75, 79
Pope, 35, 51, 63, 83
  Lewis, 77
Porter
  James, 34
Potts
  William, 57, 70, 73, 82
  Wm., 71
Pounds
  Newmon, 71
  William, 69
Powell
  Cader, 76

Stephen, 76
Pritchett
  John, 55
  Leon, 59, 60
Pyron
  Lewis, 65
Ramay
  Absalom, 40
Ramey
  A., 61, 64, 65, 73, 81, 89
  Ab., 38, 64, 68
  Abs., 5, 10, 35
  Absalem, 35, 37
  Absalom, 5, 6, 9, 10, 14, 15, 17, 18, 23, 26, 28, 32, 38, 75, 91
  Absm., 19, 24, 26, 29, 32
  Absolom, 79, 83
  Daniel, 17
  Edmund, 17
  Fanny, 17
  Nancy, 17
  Presley, 17
  Sarah, 17
  William, 8, 9, 79
  Wm., 6, 8, 9, 16, 67, 81
Raney
  Wm., 71
Ree___, 49
Reed
  William, 87
Reid
  George, 68, 83
Reynolds
  Benjamin, 10
  Busby, 33
  Harmon, 42
  Jno., 6, 7
  Joseph, 61
  Preston, 34
  Thomas, 53, 82

Thos., 83
Rice
  Benja., 30
  Benjamin, 27
  Benjn., 79
Rick
  Chs., 62
Roberson
  Wm., 77
Robertson
  David, 45
  William, 48, 50, 79, 84
  Wm., 81
Robinson
  Wm., 55
Rodgers
  Ben, 16
Roe, 69
Rogers, 92
  Baley, 52
  Dempsey, 56
  James, 46, 58
  Jas., 58
  Peley, 42, 58
  Thomas, 34, 46
  Thos., 42, 52, 58
Rolaleg
  Tho., 48
Roleghdy
  James, 48
Ross, 43, 60
  Jno., 71, 74
  John, 42, 63, 67, 73, 79
Runels
  Harmon, 90
  T., 89
Runnells, 48
Runnels, 91
  Gallant, 24
  Gallt., 20

Gartent, 33, 48
Harmon, 69, 82
Preston, 62, 91
Thomas, 69
Rutledge, 59
  Tho., 50
Sapington
  Richd., 20
Saveall
  John, 65
Sawyer
  John, 91
Scott
  Eliza, 11, 20
  Elizabeth, 8, 28
  James, 76
  Jas., 6
  John, 51
  William, 81
  Wm., 71
Scrivener
  Thos., 62
Scriviner
  Jesse, 48
Scroggin
  Humphrey, 70, 71
Scroggins
  Chatt. D., 62
  George, 49
  H., 76
  Tho., 76
Scurlock, 54
  Pressley, 47
Scutt
  John, 40
Sexton, 26
Shackleford, 90
Shannon
  Owen, 59
  Thomas, 50

Shay
  David, 5, 34
Shepperd, 89
Sherman
  John L., 57
Shields, 59, 60
  Jno., 6
  John, 50, 52, 63
  Jos., 66
  Joseph, 65
  Patrick, 67
  Thos., 67
Simons
  Joseph, 74
Simpson
  Gilbert, 49
  Rice, 49
  Robert, 52
  William, 49
Simson
  Thomas, 48
Skurlock
  Joshua, 69
  Presley, 69
  William, 69
Smith
  Alexander, 33
  James, 49
  John, 29, 47
  Johnston, 51
  Joseph, 41, 43, 53, 57, 59, 87
  William, 49
  Wm., 71
Sparks, 19
  Absalom, 26, 30, 32
  Jesse, 16
  Jessee, 6, 49
  Nathan, 21, 25
  William, 30, 32
  Wm., 6

Stathens
　Love, 38
Stathews
　Love, 39
Stean
　James, 87
Stedman, 85
Stewart
　David, 47
　Geo., 47
　George, 47
　Jas., 47
Stewert, 90
　Saml., 47
Stewrt
　Jas., 47
Stith
　William, 56
Stokes
　Montfort, 5
　Wm. M., 5, 6
Stone
　Mathew, 14, 15, 17, 22
　Wm., 35, 37, 91
Stoneham
　Henry, 50
Streatman
　Wm., 15, 25
Streetman
　Wm., 10
Strickland
　Charles, 50
　Clary, 24
　Harriet, 22
　Henry, 22, 24, 50
　Jacob, 24
　Lowness, 22
　Mary, 22, 24
　Richd., 24
　Soln., 66

　Solo., 66
Stringer
　James, 68, 78, 85
Strong, 19, 47, 48, 92
　Elijah, 77
　Jemima, 77
　Jno., 16
　John, 62
　Johnson, 8, 72, 84, 89
　Jonathan, 8
　Sherrod, 91
　Tempy, 77
　William, 8, 9, 11, 39, 79, 80, 84
　William, Jr., 8, 10
　William, Sr., 11
　Wm., 8, 9, 35, 37, 38, 67, 80, 81
　Wm., Jr., 16
　Wm., Sr., 25
Stubblefield
　William, 90
Taylor
　Archd., 49
　Arthur, 36, 42, 47, 92
　Charles, 47, 51
　Chas., 47, 65
　Chs., 66
　Edmund, 9, 11, 12, 15, 21
　G., 10
　Geo., 62, 80
　George, 49
　Robt., 47
Tegnor
　Phillip, 69
Templeton
　John, 65
　Thomas, 65, 69
　Elizabeth, 20
　Jailes, 71
　Jett, 62, 63, 64, 69
　Morrill, 91

Owen, 59
Thompson
  John, 36, 37, 41, 43
Thornton
  Prior, 91
Thurmond, 90
  David, 13, 15
  James, 61, 71
  John, 48
  Richd., 44, 68
Thweatt
  Peterson, 89
Tidwell
  Absalom, 71
  Jno., 91
  Levy, 51
Tiner
  Harris, 65
Towmend
  Eli, 52
Townsend, 52
  Henry, 66
  John, 65, 77, 84
  Levy, 57
  Thomas, 57
  Thos., 73
Townsinds
  Jno., 71
Traylor, 61, 92
  Champn. T., 34
  Randh., 23
  Randolph, 6, 19, 23, 35, 49, 91
Trent
  Henry, 6, 11, 21, 62
Truman
  John, 73
Turner
  Richard, 52, 53
  Richd., 53
Tuttle, 16, 34, 46, 61

Nicholas, 16, 34
Tweedle
  Jno., 41
Van, 46, 54, 87
Vanable
  John, 59
Vann, 46, 84
Venable
  John, 59
  Robert, 50, 52
Vermillion
  Ben, 6, 7
  Benj., 50
  Benjn., 91
Vincent
  Jesse, 43
Wadkins
  Wm., 63
Wakefield
  John, 49
Walker
  David, 86
  Horo., 49
Wall
  David, 48
Wallace
  Barthow., 67
  Geo., 21, 67
  George, 76
  James, 48
  James, Jr., 49
  Jno., 21, 22, 25, 66
  Jno., Sr., 65
  John, 49, 61, 62, 67
  John, Jr., 49, 65
  Joseph, 65
  Robt, 48
  Saml., 49
  William, 49
Waller

John, 76
Wallis
  George, 48
Walls
  John, 50
Walton, 67
Ware
  John, 36
Waters
  Mathew, 6
Watkins
  Benj., 37
  Benjn., 35, 70, 71, 91
  Jno., 65
  William, 60, 63
  Wm., 63
Watson
  Anderson, 25
  Sarah, 70
Wear
  John, 36, 44
Weatherby
  George, 41, 42
Webb
  John, 91
Welborn
  William, 49
Whaley
  Eli, 84
White, 46
  Benjamin, 49
  John, 48
Whitsell
  George, 75
Williams
  Anthony, 30, 32
  Danl., 6
  David, 47
  Edd., Sr., 71
  Edwd., 84

Henry, 10, 51
Isham, 12, 30, 32
Jonan., 49
M., 64
Paul, 48
Williamson, 41, 42
  M., 20, 38, 65, 66, 67, 68
  Micah., 38
  Micajah, 39, 65, 80
  Wm., 65, 67
Willingham
  Tho., 50
Willis
  N., 21
Willson
  G., 66
  George, 35, 68, 72
  Robt., 65, 74
  William, 86
Wilson
  Anderson, 32
  Geo., 68
  George, 29, 32, 73
  Samuel, 60
Winn
  Elisha, 39, 57
Witt, 76, 77
  David, 78, 90
Wmson
  M., 25, 31, 61
  Micajah, 35, 68, 71, 81
  Micajh., 26
Wood
  Aaron, 34, 90
  Aron, 62
  Ethd., 72
  Etheldred, 55
  Mathew, 74
  Matt, 71, 72, 78
  Matthew, 78

112

    Richd., 90
Woods
    Jno., 92
    John, 53, 69, 87
Wooten
    Bartlet, 65
    Bartley, 57
    Gilley, 57
Worthen

    Jno., 71
Wray
    Phillip, 64
Wright, 60
Wynn
    Elisha, 39, 40
Young
    Danl., 20

www.ingramcontent.com/pod-product-compliance
Lightning Source LLC
LaVergne TN
LVHW091600060526
838200LV00036B/933